LITTLE BOAT
BIG OCEAN

by

Alan Rush

Grosvenor House
Publishing Limited

This book is published by
Grosvenor House Publishing Ltd
28-30 High Street, Guildford, Surrey, GU1 3HY.
www.grosvenorhousepublishing.co.uk

A CIP record for this book
is available from the British Library

ISBN 978-1-907652-46-2

To Tamsin, for all of her hard work, encouragement and making the publishing of this book possible.

Foreword

Between my 19th and 21st years, I travelled overland to Australia and New Zealand, toured both countries extensively, and returned home by a similar route. During the course of these travels I visited such "exotic" countries as Indonesia, Laos, Nepal, Afghanistan and Iran. I arrived back in England in June 1972 suffering from malaria, hepatitis and dysentry and was promptly hospitalised.

The story actually begins in the spring of 1973 when I received a wedding invitation from a Canadian friend, who I had first met in Katmandu. At the time I found that I had only sufficient money for a one way ticket to Canada, but being 22 years old, single and totally irresponsible I decided to attend the wedding. On my arrival at Toronto international airport I was issued with a 3 month visitors permit and cautioned not to accept employment.

Two years later I was picked up by Immigration officers, held in the Waterloo County jail for 3 days and deported to England.

Being still rather a perverse individual, I decided that this was an unacceptable situation and after 6 weeks in

England I flew to the USA and drove across the border into Canada under an assumed name. This was to have been a short term jaunt, but I was not to use my own name again for over 4 years.

I travelled to British Columbia believing the wages to be higher and the climate milder on the west coast. The grass is sometimes greener and I found that the climate was indeed more temperate. My plan was to work for a year, saving as much as I could, before leaving Canada for destinations as yet undecided. Two months after my arrival in British Columbia I tore the cartilage in my left knee, had it removed and was unable to work for 3 months. The following summer, 1976, my left lung collapsed and a portion of it had to be removed, leaving me penniless once more.

By the end of 1977 I had managed to save some money and had decided to buy a sailboat on which to leave Canada and cruise the Pacific. Real ocean going yachts are expensive, my bank manager was reluctant to assist, and so it was that I bought "Balandra" in January 1978 for $3 500.00.

Balandra was a locally built wooden sloop twenty feet nine inches long, with a beam of six feet and a draft of three feet six. Although tiny and badly dilapidated, I saw in her a means to cruise the Pacific that was within my financial capabilities. The spring of 1978 was spent in restoring Balandra, and the summer was spent in learning how to sail her. I had never been aboard a sailboat until the day I bought my own!

By autumn I was ready to leave, but a week before I was to cease work, I fell from the second step of a ladder, landed awkwardly, and tore the ligaments in my right ankle. Back to the hospital for another surgical repair and another 3 months on crutches.

Thus it was that I came to leave British Columbia in April 1979 and that is where the book begins.

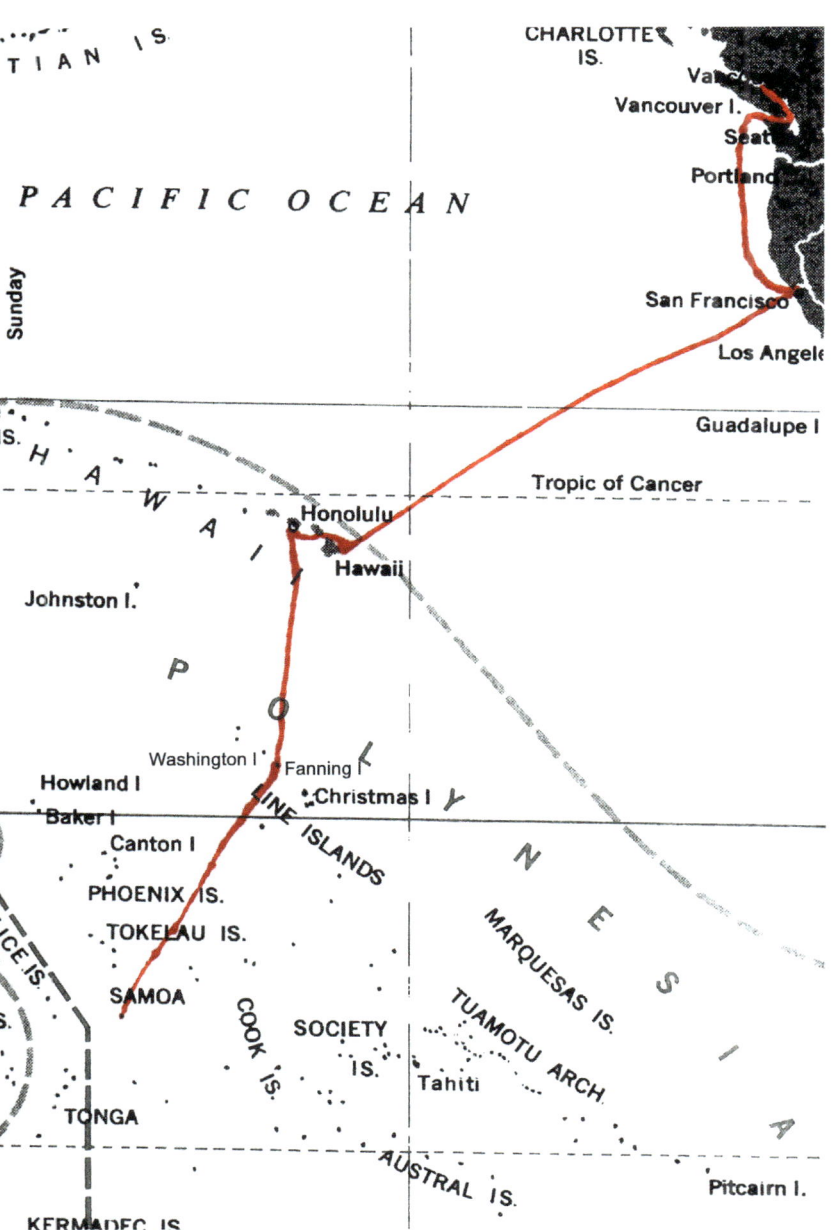

18:00 Thursday April 19th 1979, Bedwell Harbour

And so I begin. I left White Rock at 07:30 and arrived in Bedwell Harbour at 15:00. Winds in the Gulf were SE 10-12 knots, light chop on the ocean, sunshine and blue skies. Perfect sailing weather but a little cool yet. I'm the only boat in the harbour; a strong contrast to summer days filled with the chatter of children, radios and generators humming. Now everything is still but for one noisy seagull. I did a few odd jobs about the boat when I got here. Mostly trying to track down my few remaining deck leaks. Took two sets of sun sights on the way over and I'll work them out right now. 6 miles out. Not bad for such a learner. Think I'll walk up to the pub overlooking the water and have a beer or two before turning in.

19:30 Friday April 20th, Victoria Inner Harbour

Salmon for supper. I motored most of the way here over glassy seas. Covered about 30 miles, used 1.5 gallons of gas and caught 2 small salmon. Victoria feels like my first foreign port. I'm at a dock 15ft from the promenade and the imposing bulk of the Empress hotel looks benignly down upon me. Dead ahead and a half mile away, the provincial parliament building stands in its green-roofed splendour. An American tourist wanted to know if White Rock was "over there in Canada". A guy from Alberta watched with great interest as I cleaned my salmon and asked a thousand questions about sail boats and the ocean. Later he came back with his son and took some photographs of me and the boat.

12:00 Saturday April 21st, Victoria

I have just had bacon and eggs for breakfast and I'm washing it down now with a can of cold beer. I talked to some 'natives' first thing this morning and got directions to the closest liquor store. One old-timer approached me as I was standing on the dock drinking my morning 'coffee' and greeted me with "Boy that rum and coffee smells good"!!! My secret was out! I walked up to the liquor store before breakfast and bought a 40oz dark rum, a bottle of coffee liqueur (luxury for cold wet nights) and a case of beer in cans. I already have some cans in the bilge where they keep remarkably cool.

18:00. I did my last shopping and sat around the boat all afternoon drinking beer and bullshitting with passers-by. I got invited to dinner tonight aboard a 26ft power boat out of Port Angeles. Couple named Jim and Irene. Sail for Sooke in the morning.

18:00 Sunday April 22nd, Sooke Harbour

I sailed today into the dreaded (by me) Juan de Fuca Strait. I had good winds all day and it even shifted when I turned the corner through Race Passage so as to stay astern. Nearing Sooke, the seas got quite boisterous for the amount of wind and some of the more friendly waves climbed right on board, those playful little rascals. Fifty miles from here is open ocean and there is now nothing standing between us. I was met by an old man when I arrived and have talked with him for a couple of hours. He has had to give up sailing due to failing health and now commands a sturdy diesel cruiser. His name is Bill and he has given me a heave fender saying that my little things wouldn't stand up for long. He also gave me a Spanish phrase book in case I go to South America. Tomorrow he is going to take me around the harbour in his boat.

20:00 Monday April 23rd, Sooke

I tripped around Sooke basin aboard Bill's boat all morning. I talked to a man living aboard a 35ft Wharram catamaran that was junk-rigged, in more ways than one! I cleaned out the boat from end to end in the warm sunshine this afternoon. I dried everything, even the anchor line. I figure I might as well start dry. Bill won't quit giving me things.

Today he gave me a woollen scarf, a toque, a bottle of prescription painkillers, a brand new 9" x 18" Canadian flag, a plastic container with lid, an orange waistcoat (high visibility) and a can of instant soup mix that makes 60 servings. I turned down a good pair of oars, a Douglas protractor and a whetstone in a leather case. I, in turn, gave him several charts of the gulf islands that I no longer need. Westerly winds are forecast for tomorrow so I'll stay here and wait for a day or so and see what transpires. I've been in Sooke now for 28 hours but have yet to go ashore.

18:00 Tuesday April 24th, Sooke

The alarm went off at 5 a.m. and I was surprised to find it light already. I poked my head out to find the wind still steady out of the west. I made coffee, poured in a shot of rum and crawled back into bed until 07:30 (no point trying to fight the elements). Bill was down here talking to me most of the day. Today he gave me about $50-worth of blocks, shackles and sundry other fittings. As the old sailors say, "you can never have too many blocks"! I spent the day re-stowing gear again and again and again. The man on the radio says the wind will shift to the east tonight and blow briskly from there all day tomorrow. The barometer has been steady all day. Sunny and light westerly winds. I want to clear Cape Flattery, 50 miles distant, in daylight.

15:00 Thursday April 26th, Juan de Fuca Strait

Clear skies, sunshine, barometer falling slightly, light easterly winds and large waves. Balandra is steering herself right now with the twin jibs set. I think I'll call that my Gemini rig. Course 240°, position about 10-15 miles NE of Cape Flattery. The horizon is very hazy and landmarks hard to distinguish. I'm bucking a flooding tide right now and progress is slow. It turns at 17:00 and I'll still have two more hours of daylight after that. There is a lot of freighter traffic and I'm closing on the shipping lane right now. They've been averaging 2 per hour so I hope I'm well clear of them by dark. I don't plan to sleep tonight anyway. I'll keep watch and sleep in daylight tomorrow. I was up at 03:30 this morning and on my way by 05:00 so it's going to be a long day.

17:00 We just crossed a very distinct tide line so hope to have it on my side now. There is nothing now between me and China some 6,000 miles away. The wind is still light but we are moving along nicely. I haven't touched the helm since Gemini took over. It steers a straighter course downwind than I ever could. The boat rolls quite a bit but nothing I can't live with. The main problem with sailing off into the sunset is that the sails block out the sun. I just heard on the radio that there's a small craft warning in effect at Port Angeles and winds where I am are forecast as easterly 10-20 knots, maybe up to 30 tonight. I wish just a little of it would turn up soon.

21:00 The wind has picked up and we're moving well and right on course. It's difficult to go below and leave the boat to her own devices, especially at night. Everything is going so smoothly I may try to sleep for an hour at a time tonight.

Noon, Friday April 27th

Open ocean at last. The wind is light out of the south east, barometer steady, sky clear, hazy horizon towards land. To the north I can see a few snow-capped peaks poking up through the haze. There are fishing boats all around trawling, none of them come close. I slept all night last night but got up every hour or so to look around and check our course. At around 03:00, the wind shifted to the south east which, with the sails set to run dead downwind, put me on a north west course. I opted to wait for daylight before changing the sails and let her run on. There is a porpoise swimming not 50 feet away and closing. Ah, he saw me reach for the camera and left. Must be shy. So, I ran all night and am now well west of Juan de Fuca but also well north of where I want to be. The mountains I could see were on the south west coast of Vancouver Island. I'm now close-reaching, headed about south, south west and my little orange storm jib is steering. I have it set like a staysail but backed to weather with the sheet passing through a block at the shrouds, thence to a quarter block and then secured to the tiller. The tiller is held steady the other way with shock cord. It steers the boat better than I can.

20:30 I am becalmed. At around 13:00 the wind dropped to a whisper and the sails slatted wildly as I rolled so I took them in. I set them again around 17:00 and crept along for maybe a mile but now I've taken them down for the night. I'm still less than 20 miles from the SW Vancouver Island coast so I'll be watching my drift if a breeze does come up. With no sails up, we're rolling drunkenly on the swell. I think I'll go and set a riding sail to try and dampen it.

06:00 Saturday April 28th

I woke with a start to the sound of a voice calling. On looking out of the window I found a fishing boat right alongside on a still, glassy sea. I popped my bleary-eyed head out of the hatch and we talked for a while. He was anchored for the night and woke to find me drifting a quarter of a mile away so he came over to satisfy his curiosity. I, in turn, was curious about him anchoring way out here until he told me we were only 30 fathoms and he carries 140 fathoms of chain and anchor line. That's 840 feet!!! It didn't faze him at all that I was headed for San Francisco. He wished me a good trip and went back to his fishing. Today promises to be beautiful in all respects but one. No wind! The pilot chart says 2% calms for this part of the ocean in April but maybe the wind didn't read the pilot.

17:00 At around 09:00 a breeze picked up and I set sail with the storm jib set to steer us. I can't get over how well she self-steers from a close reach to a broad reach with that rig. From a broad reach to dead downwind, Gemini steers. The wind I have now is out of the south east and I'm close-reaching, course south, south west. I'm 60 miles off the US coast and 50 miles south of Vancouver Island. My navigation, by advancing lines of position, is working out very well and I take sights and work them constantly. Next I'll learn to do sun and moon fixes, then I'll move to the planets. While sailing along in the morning sunshine, I spied a small bird flying furiously to overhaul me. He came aboard without permission and perched himself on the tip of my fishing rod, a most uncertain roost as I was fishing at the time. He was a small brown finch with a splash of yellow on his head. He was a long way from land and I assume very hungry and tired as these are great tamers of all beasts. He permitted me to come very close with the camera and took some bread from my hand. On finding some dew drops, as yet undried, he drank and then explored the whole boat, nibbling on another piece of bread I put out.

After an hour's rest, being now well-fed and watered, he took flight and headed unerringly for the closest land. I wished him well and thanked him for the diversion. The sky clouded over at about noon and has yet to clear. It's quite cool outside so I've been below all afternoon. (Thank you boat for steering yourself so well). I am still making more westing than I care for but that can't be helped. The further out I get the sooner I'll pick up the current that will give me 12 miles a day. Also, further out I may pick up more northerly winds.

For myself, I feel good in health and spirits though my knees are complaining about all of the kneeling and crouching. I'm almost out of liquor but it won't hurt me to do without that for a while. I decided not to go to a liquor store till I get to San Francisco. Yesterday, whilst I was becalmed in the warm sunshine, I took off all of my clothes and washed my hair and body in the cockpit, then sat naked in the sun for a couple of hours thinking about all of the people who had told me I'd freeze my butt off going down the coast this early in the year.

18:00 A coastguard plane just passed low overhead.

19:20 The wind has again fallen very light and I'm barely maintaining steerageway. I hope it decides what it's going to do before dark.

09:00 Sunday April 29th

I am becalmed once more on a glassy, heaving sea rolling heavily on the swell. I had to get up at 22:00 last night and take the sails down as they were slatting back and forth as we rolled. With no sails up she rolled badly all night, beam on to the swells and I slept little. At 06:00 there was a light breeze out of the south east and I set sail course south, south west. Within an hour the wind had shifted around until my course was a little north of west so I came about which meant resetting the steering sail. I just got her set up on course, heading almost true south, right where I want to go and the wind died right away. There is a little breeze now out of the south west but not enough to fool me into setting sail. I saw and heard a killer whale pass me by in the distance this morning. I spent the day reading, writing and listening to a very faint Vancouver Island radio station.

18:00 The wind picked up out of the west at 15:00 and within an hour it was blowing briskly. Now we'll put some miles behind us. In the 24 hours before 15:00 we had covered only 6 miles.

19:30 I put a reef in the mainsail as the weather helm was getting the better of the steering sail. We still have the jenny up and we're moving well. It's blowing about 15 knots from the west and we're headed due south.

12:00 Monday April 30th

It's blowing like hell out there. The wind continued to increase all night and by 03:00 was in excess of 20 knots so I donned oilskins and took in the jenny and the steering sail. It was difficult to tell the state of the sea in the dark. With the reefed main sheeted in and the helm lashed down she made her way slowly to windward south west so I let her carry on until daybreak. At first light I took down the main and she now lies ahull. The wind is in excess of 30 knots with seas 6-8 feet and breaking. The odd one breaks heavily on deck and against the cabin side and the motion is incredible. She's taking a pounding but I guess she's built for it. My nagging anxieties have not yet degenerated into actual fear.

20:00 The wind is still moaning in the rigging as another day with no progress nears its end. With each wave she rolls her mast to leeward and, as the wave passes under, flicks back to windward, the wind in the rigging fluctuating with the whipping of the mast. Each way she rolls, she submerges her toerail. I hear the breaking waves hissing towards me for a few seconds before they hit and I brace myself. Some break against the hull with a loud slap and push us sideways through the water. Others go right over the top. So far just a few drops have come in through the edge of the main hatch. I managed to spill a whole cupful of boiling water while making tea using my gimballed propane stove. I tried to turn her bow into the wind with the storm jib set as a riding sail on the backstay and an improvised sea anchor streamed from the bow. Nothing doing. She remains obstinately beam on to the wind and waves. I did not sleep at all last night due to the motion and I feel very tired. The way we are rolling now is still not very conducive to restful sleep. I figure I'm about 100 miles off the US coast, down around latitude 47°20'N and being pushed just south of east at 1 knot or less.

09:00 Tuesday May 1st

The wind increased still more during the night and I got brief snatches of sleep between the bigger waves, very brief. I lay in bed until 08:00 as there was little else to be done. I went to pour milk in my coffee but it's all turned to butter! The sun is shining in a clear blue sky and the barometer is high and steady. I think I'll take some sights and see where I am. Then I'll maybe hoist a scrap of sail and see what happens.

18:30 By about noon the wind had passed its peak and was down to around 25-30 knots. I double-reefed the mainsail and even reefed the working jib, then set the storm jib to steer. This all took me about one and a half hours as the seas were still very high, 12-15 feet or more, and I was holding on with everything but my teeth. Within a couple of hours I shook one reef out of the main and unreefed the jib. Now the wind is about 10-15 knots but I'll leave the other reef in overnight just in case. The wind is now out of the west and I'm beam-reaching due south. The barometer is steady and set at 1020. The temperature inside the boat is usually between 50 and 60° F. A freighter passed within about half a mile of me this afternoon, the first one I've seen for a couple of days. He was headed west. The seas have gone down considerably so maybe tonight I'll get some sleep.

12:00 Wednesday May 2nd

I slept well until about 04:00 when I was awakened by the sails slatting back and forth. Becalmed again. I got up and took down the jib and sheeted the main in tight. The oil lamp on the backstay had gone out but as we were only an hour or so from daybreak I let it be. I went back to bed only to be awoken an hour later to find we were moving through the water again. With the main sheeted in she was steering herself in a fresh breeze to the north west. Wrong way lady. I got up again and reset the sails, course south east. I had to bribe my body to get up out of my warm bed into the chilly dawn air and consequently I got to lay in bed until 08:30 and then have scrambled eggs for breakfast. The wind is now very light out of the south and I replaced the jib with the jenny. She's now pointing as high as she'll go and I'm still making too much easting.

18:00 I am once more becalmed. All day I have been sailing slowly, close-hauled, course south east and I'm now about 60 miles from the mouth of the Columbia River. I washed my hair and body this afternoon and was that water ever cold! I've had my fishing line rigged all day but to no avail and now it hangs lifeless, straight down.

21:00 I heard a splash alongside and poked my head out of the hatch to see something about 3 feet long, swimming alongside. I thought it was a large fish and was reaching for my harpoon when it stuck its head up to breath! It was a seal and I watched quietly as it swam all around the boat and carefully explored the 200 feet of poly line that I tow astern, rolling right over it and mouthing it. When it decided there was nothing to eat, it left.

09:30 Thursday May 3rd

Last night at 22:00 I poked my head outside to find a breeze blowing and a freighter about a mile away. I got the sails up and stayed on deck until well clear of my lumbering neighbour. At 01:00 I had to get up and take the sails down again. I stayed in bed until a breeze came up at 08:30 then got us under way.

13:00 It's blowing well now. Unfortunately it's a south wind and I'm over on my ear beating into the south east. I'll have to come about onto an offshore tack before dark as I'm closing in on the coast. I've only covered about 15 miles since 18:00 yesterday. I just put a reef in the main and the wind is still increasing. I'll give it one more hour then change tacks to get some sea room in case it really blows.

14:00 Took in the jenny and set the working jib.

15:00 I put her over on an offshore tack and put a second reef in the main. Even with that her rail is well under and she's moving fast. The seas are up around 6-8 feet and it's a very rough ride. The boat's interior is a mess. When I changed tacks, a shelf full of unsecured books spread themselves randomly throughout the boat. The best course I can make on this tack is just west of south west. The radio keeps fluctuating as I rise and fall on the waves.

18:00 Looks like another sleepless night coming up. We're still pounding our way to windward with waves continually washing over the length of the boat. An occasional deep roll puts the leeward windows underwater.

20:00 I've taken down the jib and steering sail. It's blowing over 30 knots with seas 8-10 feet. With the amount of solid water coming on deck, my weak spots let in drips and dribbles of water here and there. I was able to light the kerosene stove and I'm now drying some of my damp items including bedding. I have the double-reefed main still up and sheeted in tight. The motion is much easier than hulling and I still have way on to windward. Still I can feel the shuddering in the rigging through the hull and cannot decide whether to leave it up all night. It's also pouring with rain – the first of the trip. I could use a drink or three!

08:00 Friday May 4th

I left the reefed main up all night and it came to no harm. It blew and raged and rained all night long but the morning bought sunshine and light winds. Very light and out of the south. The seas are still quite large and continually roll the wind out of the sails.

Noon. Beating to windward is a miserable way to sail. I now have the jenny up, the rail down and I'm making a little south of south west. The wind is blowing around 10 knots but the swells are still large from last night. I have various items hung in the rigging to dry.

13:00 I've just worked out my position and I'm 10 miles north west of where I was this time yesterday!!! Maybe I would have made less leeway with the main down. This could get to be frustrating. I've covered only 60 miles to the south in the last 3 days. Good thing I have plenty of food on board. Speaking of which, I just found 2 cans of beer while digging through the bilge.

14:00 Here we go again. Wind and seas starting to build. I put a reef in the main and replaced the jenny with the working jib then put a second reef in the main. The wind has lifted a little less water over the bow while still headed south west. Now I'm going to drink my beer.

19:00 Now I'm laying ahull again with the wind blowing about 30 knots. I was starting to feel more like a submarine than a sailboat, going right through most of the waves. I've streamed a large plastic pail from the bow and set a riding sail on the backstay but she stays beam on to the seas and the motion is most uncomfortable. It's pouring with rain so I think I'll stay home tonight. The barometer has fallen considerably in the last few hours and is now at 1000 millibars.

08:00 Saturday May 5th

What a night, what a wild insane night. The wind right now is about 30 knots, waves 12-15 feet and that's a great improvement. All night the wind shrieked and howled in the rigging and wave after wave broke over Balandra, several times swamping the cockpit. The force of the waves squeezed water through every imaginable (and some unimaginable) crack and hole, especially around the hatches. And the rain! I haven't seen rain like that since I was in the tropics. The drumming of it on the deck and cabin would compete with the wind and the roar of breaking water. This morning the sun is shining and if the wind and seas go down a little more I'll string stuff up in the rigging to dry for a while before getting under way. Everything is wet. Bedding, towels, my charts and books. I'm almost afraid to take any sights as I'm sure I've been pushed way north again. I wonder whatever happened to the north west winds that are supposed to blow 60% of the time here at this time of year.

I just heard on the radio that there is a gale warning in effect on the coast with winds of 45 knots and above but it is supposed to moderate by this afternoon. One thing that surprised me last night was that I was not as scared as I'd thought I would be. I was annoyed at all of the water coming in and that I couldn't get any sleep. I have a lot of confidence in my boat and knew nothing much could happen to us.

19:00 I'll never make it unless the wind shifts. I'm once more beating to windward in 20 knots of wind and large waves. The boat and I are taking quite a pounding. I spent some time today trying to seal the hatches a little better but I'm still taking in some water. Everything is damp and I have no way of drying any of it. When I fixed my position this morning I found I had indeed been pushed all the way back to where I started yesterday morning. I'll try to keep going all through tonight though it will mean no sleep again. One consolation is that the wind has shifted around to the south west so I'm able to steer a fairly southerly course. In the past 8 days I've only covered some 160 miles. It's very discouraging. I knew this first part of the trip would be tough but I never thought it would be this bad. I'm glad I'm doing it alone. Sue couldn't have hacked it I'm sure and I don't think I could have done either with someone else jammed in here with me. I just peeked outside and I think the wind has dropped a little. I swear some of those waves are 20-25 feet high, they're monstrous.

08:00 Sunday May 6th

This is truly miserable. Now I know why it's called BEATING to windward. This isn't sailing, it's full scale war. By 22:00 last night I could take no more and I took down the jib and steering sail. I left the double-reefed main up to steady the motion so that I could get some much needed sleep and crawled into my damp sleeping bag in my damp clothes. During the night it rained and rained and blew and rained. This morning conditions are much the same, 20-25 knots out of the SW and I'm pounding into it making a little east of south. If conditions don't moderate by about noon, I'll head offshore again and when I have enough sea room I'll lie ahull until the wind shifts. Even though I might end up in Alaska while waiting. It's too rough right now to take any sights. In fact it's too rough to do anything but hang on.

14:00 I'm heading offshore with sheets eased a little, course due west. The wind and seas are much the same. Sunny periods are interrupted by torrential rain. The wind is supposed to drop to 10-15 knots and shift to the west tomorrow. The man on the radio said so and I believe him. I hung some damp towels in the rigging today and it promptly rained and turned them into wet towels.

18:00 We're still heading due west and on this course I'm not taking so much water over the bow. Before sundown I'll drop the jib and steering sail and again leave the double-reefed main up for the night. Since I can't get to the south, I may as well sleep. I'm very tired, not only from lack of sleep but from the constant heeling and pounding, the bracing and hanging on and the frustration of going on day after day and getting nowhere. I'm getting very short-tempered and when things happen, I scream and swear at the waves, the wind, the sails, whatever is the object of my misery. It's stupid and it doesn't even make me feel any better but I can't control it. Sometimes at night in bed I'll look out of the window and see another sailboat sailing by. Then I'll realise that I'm lying down and can't see out of the window from this position. Another popular trick of the imagination is to conjure up hazards like rocks or ships or being able to see the bottom because the water is so shallow. These 'visions' occur at night somewhere between sleeping a waking.

11:00 Monday May 7th

At about 23:00 last night the wind fell very light and the rain fell very hard. At midnight, when the rain stopped and the wind picked up again it had shifted maybe 20° westward. I got up and dropped the jib and steering sail and put her about on the other tack. With the double-reefed main up she moved slowly south and I left her like that and went back to bed. Whilst on deck doing this, I saw a very strange sight. Floating a foot or so beneath the surface was what, in shape, appeared to be a loop of heavy rope, maybe 20 feet long but doubled back on itself. It glowed a bright luminous green, not phosphorescence but vivid glowing green like the numbers on my alarm clock. It was soon left astern and I have no idea what it could have been.

My top-of-the-range, expensive 90 amp hour battery is very low already. That's very disappointing as I've only had the running lights on for about 5 nights. I just use them when it's too windy for the kerosene lamp as it is now. It'll be kerosene or nothing from now on. This morning the wind and seas were down a little but the wind is now over 20 knots again. I'm still having to point fairly high to make a southerly course but I am at last headed the right way. I'm hoping the wind will continue to shift westerly and maybe go down just a little. I've had two reefs in the main for days upon days now. I feel like today is a turning point and that things will take an upward trend now. To celebrate I scrambled my last 3 eggs for breakfast and dried the seat of my pants over the stove. I pulled up the floor and mopped several gallons of water out of the bilge. I picked out a few cans of food and joy of joys I found 3 more cans of beer! They are definitely the last.

The wind is getting very gusty and we get knocked down and rounded up into the wind, then fall off again with a great deal of flogging.

22:00 All day we pounded our way south through steep choppy seas in brisk winds. It was overcast all day and rained much of the time. I stayed below, ate peanuts drank beer and read. We took just enough water on board to keep things damp. No fire hazard on my boat! The radio station I've been listening to for the past week is finally, finally, beginning to fade. Hurray for progress.

08:00 Tuesday May 8th

Another miserable and sleepless night has passed. The wind would die and I'd get up and sheet everything in tight to stop the sails slatting. Minutes later it would be gusting to 20-25 knots and we'd be on our ear and I'd get up and slacken off the sheets. I repeated this maybe six times; at one stage taking the jib down then putting it back up 5 minutes later. Since the early hours, the wind has held and we're close-reaching into the south, going like a train. The wind is 20, gusting 30 knots and wave after wave comes over the bow as we slam and pound into them. Each wave deposits a cupful of water through the forward hatch and the bilge is again full. My sleeping bag is no longer damp, it's soaked. I literally had to dry myself when I got up this morning, being in bed was like taking a passive shower. If the sun comes out today I'll take down the sails and try to get things dried out a little.

11:00 It's blowing in excess of 30 knots with large seas running. The sky is heavily overcast and it's cold. I took down the jib and I'm moving slowly south under double-reefed main and steering sail. The motion is a lot easier but I still take the occasional wave right over the top. No way to dry anything, I can't even light the kerosene stove as it's so rough. I hope this moderates before nightfall or it will be another wet, miserable night. Nothing to do but sit and wait.

15:30 If I'd know this trip was going to be so hard I doubt that I would ever have begun. It's just as well I didn't know. This is by far the hardest thing I've ever done in a life that has been far from empty. Well I'm committed, so best I stop bitching. The wind is still blowing and the seas are up around 20 feet. The sun came out for a while and I decided to have another try at sealing the fore hatch. I stuffed in more rags and covered everything with masking tape and I can see no place for water to enter. I had finished and was just standing up when I saw the wave. It towered above me with its crest just starting to topple. As we rose to meet it, I jumped up onto the cabin top and clung to the mast. It broke right over the boat hitting me at waist level and filling the cockpit. The main hatch was closed but one door was open and a couple of gallons snuck inside. My pillow had been the only item of bedding I'd managed to keep dry. I now have no pants that are even close to dry.

19:00 It must be blowing 50 knots out there. I just took down the steering sail but have left the double-reefed main up. I can't face the thought of spending the night pitching about broadside onto these huge seas. I've spread the old jib over the wet rug to sit and sleep on. My efforts with the forward hatch seem to have helped. I can think of nothing better right now than to go to sleep and not wake up until dawn, then at dawn, to find clear skies and the wind out of the north at 15 knots. If I believed in God I'd pray for it.

09:00 Wednesday May 9th

Well the sun is shining and the wind, though blowing lustily, is out of the north west. If it drops a few knots we'll be in good shape. Maybe today is the turning point. The boat and I are a mess. I spent an uncomfortable night wrapped in a cold and clammy sail and slept little. Just after dark last night I had to take down the main as the wind continued to increase. The sea was like a living thing gone mad. The barometer has climbed considerably in the last 24 hours. I hope it means a change in the weather.

19:00 Heaven, joy ecstasy. 15 knots of wind out of the north and sunshine all day. Gemini is steering and we've put away about 40 miles since noon. I'm dry! My bedding is dry and the foam and rug are trying hard. I'm sitting in the cockpit, the first time this month. This morning, while kneeling on the bow hanking on the jib, a killer whale surfaced alongside, not 10 feet from my left elbow. Beneath the surface it cut across the bow and passed down the starboard side. I could see its white parts easily through the clear water. I hustled back into the boat and grabbed my camera. Nothing like a camera to scare whales away. There were at least two of them and they made numerous passes close to Balandra but only surfaced one more time. I was more scared than I had ever been in the Gulf but that was in part because I could see them clearly beneath the surface and see how close they came. Half an hour later they were still around but wouldn't come up for photos so I hoisted the twins and got out of there. At first the following seas were so large that Balandra's stern kept getting thrown way off course. The seas are down somewhat now, though she still steers a zig zag course.

11:30 Thursday May 10th

I'm now in Californian waters under a clear sky with wind at 15 knots out of the north. Last night I slept through to 06:00 with only one awakening. Gemini could not have been kinder. Already it feels like the last week and a half were but a bad dream. North winds are forecast through today and tonight at 10-20 knots. If it holds for one more day I'll be looking for Noonday Rock by Saturday afternoon. The eternal optimist.

20:00 We're still flying south under clear skies and, as the sun set, a bright full moon rose to light my way. Noon yesterday until noon today we covered 110 miles. From May 1st to May 6th I also covered 110 miles! I opened a whole canned chicken for supper to celebrate my change of fortune.

09:30 Friday May 11th

Unbelievable. In the last 24 hours we've put away 130 miles, that's over 5 knots average. We're right on course and I haven't touched the helm or the sails since I set them up 2 days ago. The wind has picked up a little overnight to 15-20 knots and we're flying. The waves throw the stern around a little but our course averages out and we're really making knots. At this speed I could conceivably be in San Francisco by Saturday night but I don't think I can get cleared until Monday without paying a $25 overtime fee. We'll see how we do today, I don't want to be messing around the Bay entrance in the dark. I've covered as many miles in the last 2 days as I did in the ten days from April 28th!

16:00 The wind has continued to increase and is probably close to 30 knots by now. The seas have also really built up and Gemini is having some trouble steering. Still, we're moving fast and in the right direction so I'm not prepared to quit just yet. One wave climbed over the transom and temporarily took over the cockpit. Another slewed us around broadside on and then its pal came right behind before Gemini straightened us out and tried to roll us right over. One of the cabinets spewed its contents all over the floor. Still, the sun is shining and it's warm and dry. The barometer is steady and high so I think the wind is a passing thing. I've seen two jet planes high overhead today so I must be somewhere close to civilization. The thought occurred to me today that I've had no way to check my position and for all I really know I could be halfway to China. If I don't see land by late tomorrow I'll be starting to sweat. I just heard on the radio a forecast for fog around San Francisco Bay. I thought I was early enough in the year to avoid that.

18:45 Running downwind is deceptive. Now I'm stopped, I find the wind is over 30 knots. I pushed her too hard for too long and I paid the price and learned my lesson. My nice new whisker pole snapped where it joins the mast and I came on deck just in time to see it drifting away. Both jibs were flogging wildly and I wrestled them down, by which time the whisker pole was long gone. I'm laying ahull now and will wait until the wind diminishes.

09:00 Saturday May 12th

The ocean is back to its bad old ways. The wind continued to increase through yesterday evening and night and it is now blowing around 40 knots. The seas are up around 15 feet or more. I'm only about 130 miles from San Francisco and while laying ahull, I'm getting pushed south. The sun is shining in a clear sky and the temperature in the mid-70°s is forecast in

San Francisco. Nothing on the radio about this wind, it's supposed to be blowing 10-20 knots.

16:30 This is most tedious. The conditions haven't moderated at all and I've spent the day below eating, reading and napping. In San Francisco right now they have 79°F and no wind. So close and yet so far away. At least I am drifting in the right direction and this can't continue too much longer. I'm taking a little water through the main hatch when the odd wave comes over the top.

12:45 Sunday May 13th

The wind is still howling and I stayed in bed until noon as there was nothing else to be done. I went to bed last night at around 21:00 and it was blowing about 40 knots then. At midnight I woke suddenly to find Balandra on her side and water squirting in around the companionway doors and main hatch. I had an instant vision of her rolling right over but she righted slowly and then I thought I'd better get those sails down! There were, of course, no sails up. I was already laying ahull and what more could I do. I switched on the flashlight and surveyed the gallon or so of water sprayed all over and listened to the water slopping around in the cockpit as it slowly drained. This was intolerable, something had to be done. I put on my safety harness and clambered outside in nothing but t-shirt and boots. The wind had increased and the seas were high under a full moon. The first wave hitting my bed-warmed body left me gasping. The second had me wide awake and paying attention. I took the 200 foot safety line from astern and fastened it to the bow cleat. Unshackling the orange storm jib I gathered its 3 corners together to make a scoop shape and fastened the other end of the safety line to the corners. Groping blindly in the lazarette, I found the 10 pound lead kellet and fastened it to one corner of the sail then lowered my 'instant' sea anchor over the side. It helped but not much. The bow came up onto the wind by about 20° but it was all I could do right then. I went below, soaked and shivering, dried my body and made some hot chocolate. When I get to San Francisco I'll buy a real sea anchor. Balandra is too low to lay broadside to breaking seas of any size. She has continued to take a pounding with some water coming through the main hatch but no more bad knock downs. The wind is now down to 40 knots with an overcast sky.

18:30 The wind has increased a little and it's still overcast. I donned oilskins this afternoon and went outside for the first time in two days. I hauled in my sea anchor and it was a mess. Having no swivels and being laid line it was hopelessly snarled and tangled. The line was chaffed right through in one place and only a backup line I'd rigged prevented the loss of the sail and weight. I untangled it but did not reset it as it was of dubious value and I can't afford to lose my steering sail. The seas are huge, as big as houses and the wind is so strong it's hard to face it and breath. I sat in the cockpit for a while and watched the ocean. I wish it would quit so I could get to San Francisco. I'll be better prepared when I leave there as I now know what to expect. I battened everything down, put the cockpit cover on and came back inside. All I can do now is wait and hope it ends soon.

09:00 Monday May 14th

The conditions outside have not moderated at all. The conditions inside have deteriorated considerably. Everything is once more damp and getting damper by the day. I haven't been able to get a sun sight since Friday but I assume that I've drifted a long way south, maybe 60 miles. The ocean current here should be giving me half a knot and I'm making at least that much again in leeway. If I don't get sailing soon I'll drift past San Francisco and have to beat back up to it. I'm going to rig the storm jib today and stand to the helm to see if I can make some easting. The wind may be lighter near the coast. The coastal radio stations are saying nothing about wind.

14:00 The sun just peaked through a gap in the solid cloud cover for about 30 seconds and I squeezed off a very quick and uncertain sight. The book says 'any sight is better than none' but I'm not so sure. It gives me a line of position further south than I had guessed and I'll have to make good an easterly course. The wind is still up and the seas huge. I have the storm jib set and, with the helm lashed, we're moving slowly north east. I figure with our southerly drift she should actually be making an east course. I don't know how far offshore I am but I would guess around 60 miles.

19:00 I wish this weather would break. I've been ahull for 3 days and nights now and the wind hasn't been under 40 knots. I got another hurried and hazy sun sight to give me a dubious fix. I'm moving slowly east under storm jib with Noonday Rock 50 miles ahead (I hope). I'll let her go all night and see what tomorrow brings. If the wind subsides at all I'll get some sails up in the morning at first light and head in. I can't drift around out here forever.

10:00 Tuesday May 15th

My body is stiff and aching. I spent a cold, damp night in my clothes with water coming in around the main hatch as waves broke over us. One wave spun Balandra right around and put her on a south west course. I had to get up and come about. The cloud cover is broken here and there and I got one sight this morning. This puts me 50 miles offshore but I don't know where, north or south. The wind is still around 40 knots with large seas.

15:00 At last. I see land!!!

00:00 At 23:00 I dropped the hook in 35 feet of water in Drake's Bay, named after Sir Francis Drake who anchored here in 1579. I'll go back to this morning as I have had a fairly full day. I got under way at around 10:30 with double-reefed main and storm jib. It was still blowing about 40 knots but she wasn't too hard to handle off of the wind. I had figured out my probable drift since the previous day and accordingly steered a little north of east on a broad reach; very broad. Within an hour of taking the helm the wind lost some of its weight and the sky cleared, as if they resigned themselves to the fact that I was going to sail anyway.

Old Mr Ocean was not so soft, he kept those huge breaking seas barrelling down on my stern. I switched to the working jib and poled it out on the same side as the main. We were far enough downwind that Gemini could have steered except for the lost whisker pole. I tried wing and wing but jibed her twice before deciding it wasn't feasible in those seas. Jibing in 30 knots, even with the main double-reefed is kind of scary. The wind went down to 15-20 knots and I shook a reef out of the main. It was pleasant sailing for a while in the sunshine. The first time I'd taken the helm in 3 weeks. At 15:00 I saw my first piece of land. I dropped the sails and took a sun sight, noticing as I did the mass of grey cloud moving up fast astern. Once again I got only one sight and I had to work against the one taken earlier this morning. It showed me to be 15-20 miles north of where I wanted to be and, as I'd been steering somewhat northerly and had seen a freighter well to the south of me earlier, I accepted this position quite readily. I speculated that the headland I could see was Bodega Head. So I headed south.

After a couple of hours I hadn't sighted Reyes Point but, as the light failed, I became aware of a flashing light on the diminishing Bodega Head. On counting the flashes and checking the chart, I discovered that Bodega Head was in fact

Reyes Point. I carefully read the description on the pilot book and there was no doubt in my mind. So my original theorizing and course had been right. I came about and headed back at 18:00, beam-reaching into the north east. The wind had been building again for a while and was by this time a good 30 knots and more in the gusts. I should have put the second reef back in the main but I didn't. There was a lot of weather helm but we flew on regardless and when we surfed diagonally down the faces of those huge breaking seas I couldn't even guess at our speed.

By 21:30 it was full dark with heavy cloud cover. Steering by a flashing light on a buoy, I rounded the end of Point Reyes and entered Drake's Bay. It was pitch dark except for a few shore lights and a cloud of phosphorescence about us and trailing astern like some magical garment. The problem was to get in far enough for a good amount of scope without going on the beach. I tacked cautiously back and forth for a long time, taking bearings and being sure of my position. We finally sailed boldly in and at a pre-determined spot, dropped sails and lowered the anchor. 35 feet, perfect. I'm not sleeping tonight but sitting by the kerosene stove eating, drinking tea and coffee, listening to the radio, writing this log and being warm. There is so little motion in here and it's a treat to be able to use the stove. At first light I'll get shipshape and sail the final 20 miles to the Golden Gate bridge.

05:30 Wednesday May 16th

I've just been hit by 2 fishing boats 10 minutes apart. I'll fill in the details tomorrow.

17:30 Thursday May 17th

Yesterday morning, despite my best intentions, I fell asleep at around 04:00, still in my oilskins. I was awakened at 05:00 to find Balandra moving through the water at about 7 knots!!

I was on deck very quickly to find a fishing boat had hooked my anchor line with his stabilizer as he passed. The oil lamp on the backstay had gone out and he hadn't seen me. The guy on the fishing boat didn't understand why I was following him and yelling loudly for him to stop. He stopped and disentangled me and, other than my nerves, nothing was damaged. He went on his way muttering about people who don't have lights on their boats. I discovered that all of the shore lights I had seen were in fact fishing boats at anchor and they were all getting under way so I went below to get the battery lantern to put on the backstay although, by this time, it was getting light and visibility was several hundred feet. As I came out with the light I spotted a fishing boat 100 yards away coming right at me. He was headed right for my starboard shrouds as I jumped up on deck waving my arms and yelling lustily. He saw me at the last second and sheared off, striking my pulpit. The pulpit absorbed the worst of the blow scraping along his hull and finally being wrenched loose. His stabiliser was high enough to clear the mast but one of the lines attached to it hooked over it and, as he passed, began to heel her over. As she heeled, the line slid up the jumper stay until arrested by the masthead light. He then

dragged me sideways by the masthead for a short distance until the masthead light broke off with a metallic 'ting' and hung there lopsidedly.

All this of course took place in about 2 seconds. The man stopped and was very apologetic and I'm sure he felt terrible about the whole thing but there was nothing that could be done. At the time I wasn't angry I just felt sick and dizzy. Now, in retrospect, I'm thankful for the small amount of damage I sustained. If he had seen me one second later he probably would have sunk me or, at the very least, I would have lost my rig. He went on his way muttering about people who don't have lights on their boats. I promptly hung the battery lamp on the backstay. I should add that through both incidents there was a light on in the cabin and the curtains were open. I took the twisted remains of the pulpit, stashed it below and started to get things shipshape in the growing light. I pulled the motor out from its spot under the cockpit and got it fuelled up and ready to go.

Full daylight revealed the thing I had feared. Fog. San Francisco had 15 miles of open water to cross then along the coast for 5 miles or more. I had a couple of scares with breakers appearing dead ahead and too close for comfort and times of great doubt but, when the fog began to clear at 13:00, I was where I wanted to be. I sailed under the Golden Gate bridge at 15:00 and was tied up at the Municipal Marina half an hour later. I phoned customs and immigration and they both told me to come into town and see them but it was too late that day. I then went to the store and bought a bottle of rum, came back to the boat and drank two thirds of it. I phoned Janie and spoke at length to her and the three girls. This morning I had the most outrageous hangover but I took 2 aspirin with a couple of rum and coffees and set out to get cleared. The customs man gave me a lot of static for not having cleared before I left Vancouver. I played dumb and filled out all of his forms and promised to clear here before I go on to Hawaii. Then on to immigration which had me a little scared. My passport had nothing in it except a stamp to say I entered the States 4 years ago. From then until now, Alan Rush hadn't existed. The lady I spoke to was so fascinated by my trip and doubtless dazzled by my charm and noticed nothing. She gave me a 4 month permit to carry me right through to Hawaii.

So, Alan Rush is now officially back in the land of the living and it feels good. It sounds strange to hear people use my name and I have to watch myself when I sign things. Janie told me yesterday that Pacific Yachting wants to do an article about me. Fame at last. I spent this afternoon doing laundry, drying things and drinking beer. My legs are really sore and my knees swollen after all this unaccustomed walking. I'm still very tired generally but a couple of good night's sleep will fix me right up.

19:00 Friday May 18th

I stayed in bed until 10:00 then, as I was cooking breakfast, Don and Henry came visiting. They live on their boats down here and we soon got into the rum and coffee. We went to Don's boat when the rum was finished and drank vodka and coffee until 16:00. I then walked over to Fisherman's Wharf for a look at the marine supply stores. I said goodbye this evening to the people on 'Telcontar' who are heading back to Vancouver tomorrow morning. This evening Don is cooking dinner on his boat.

22:00 Saturday May 19th

I wrote reams of letters today. Actually only 3 but the longest was 14 pages. I did little else. Another Canadian boat came in this afternoon. Her name is 'Grog' and I'd like to talk to her people. I've talked to very few sailing people since getting in and that's a disappointment. I had to get Don and Henry to back off a little. They both came over this morning and wanted to sit and drink and chat all day again. I had to make it very clear to them that today I was doing my own thing by myself and I'd see them later. I walked up to Chestnut Street this evening where there are bars, restaurants and stores and, although the bars were all full there were no people on the streets. Saturday evening!! The bars all looked too dark and quiet or too bright and loud so I came back to Balandra and had a drink sitting on the dock. Cheaper too!

23:00 Sunday May 20th

I started on the big clean up today. I scrubbed the deck with comet and washed everything down with fresh water, including the lines. I sanded and painted the toe rail and aft hatch and sanded and varnished the coamings. I went grocery shopping this evening with some misgivings. Although I had been told it was so, I found it hard to accept that Safeways would be open until 9pm on a Sunday. I walked the mile to the store and it was open. The other six days of the week they stay open until midnight!

23:00 Monday May 21st

I sanded and varnished the cabin today. I walked over to where 'Grog' is tied up and met the people aboard her. I had supper with them and spent the evening. They are going down to Los Angeles then across to Hawaii and eventually on to New Zealand so I may run into them again.

Tuesday May 22nd

I spent the day in Sausalito. There is no moorage there for a reasonable price so I'll stay put. I walked through every street in town and sampled a good cross-section of bars. Bussed back to the boat and drank vodka with Don all evening.

Wednesday May 23rd

I painted a fair piece of the deck today and inside the cockpit. Every day I walk to Safeways and bring back an armful of groceries. Bit by bit I'm restocking and I hope to have 3 months worth of food aboard before I leave. I think I'll leave before very long. I caught three crabs and a rock cod off the dock today.

Thursday May 24th

I now have about half of the deck finished and the varnishing is all done. I caught three more crabs today. A guy from the yacht club across the harbour came over and introduced himself and offered me the use of the clubhouse and showers as his guest.

Friday May 25th

I finished the bulk of the painting. I paid for my berth for one more week and think I'll leave when that's up. A fisherman gave me a three-foot shark for crab bait but I cut a couple of fillets off it first. I gave one to Don and had the other for dinner. That old shark had 3 baby sharks inside her ready to come out. I went over to the Golden Gate Yacht Club this evening and had my first hot shower since leaving White Rock. I sat in the bar until 23:00 drinking beer.

Saturday May 26th

I varnished a few dozen assorted cans of food today ready to stow in the dark recesses of the bilge. I did a few touristy things including a visit to the Exploratorium with all its nifty space age toys. It's like a modern day Science Museum. I have a hard time shaking Don off these days. He arrives at my dock by 09:00 every day and sticks like glue while I answer in monosyllables and look engrossed in whatever I'm doing. I made two trips to Safeway today and I now have probably 2 months of food aboard.

Sunday May 27th

I hoisted myself up the mast today as far as the spreaders. I used a panel from the floor as a bosun's chair, shackled one end of the main sheet tackle to it and hoisted the other end aloft with the jib halyard which I secured. Hauling on the main sheet, I went aloft with little effort and was able to cleat it as I climbed. I shackled a wire strop in place at the spreaders and measured from it to the ring bolt on deck. I'll get a stay made up that I can fly my steering sail on but that I can secure at the foot of the mast for normal sailing. I stowed all of the cans and have room for more yet. Canned goods will be hard to get further south and more expensive. I pulled out and aired all of the sails and scrubbed out the bow section. I cleaned, filled and stowed the 5 gallon water container. Busy ain't I.

I'm getting excited about leaving and am starting to move into high gear. My fishing friend gave me two more sharks today. He gave me two yesterday as well. I've been eating the sharks and not even trying for crabs but I'm a little tired of shark after 3 days in a row. Don is fascinated by my speed and skill in gutting and filleting fish and cleaning crabs. The truth is that I do it fast to get it over with and we've had enough meat not to have to be too fussy. An older guy who, with his son, was tuning his rigging came over and asked me to feel his shrouds and tell him if they were tight enough. He must have figured that I must know what I'm doing to have gotten here. A kid fishing on the dock knocked my pulpit off into the water. I made a grapple with my gaff and got the pulpit out of 15 feet of murky water on the second sweep. I was glad I got it so easily as the kid was feeling terrible about putting me to all of this trouble.

Monday May 28th

I was working on the boat this morning when a sail boat sailed up to my dock with the helmsman calling my name. It was Mike Webber who had introduced me to the yacht club, on his 26 foot folkboat 'Ingrid' with three girls aboard. They asked if I'd like to go sailing with them for the day and I put down my tools and jumped aboard. It was blowing about 15 knots and we had a boisterous romp out under the Golden Gate Bridge against wind and tide. We then turned and ran with wind and tide astern, into Richard's Bay and Sausalito. Out of the wind it was very hot and we ghosted up to a dock and tied up for lunch. They had various chesses, cold meats, canned fish, crackers etc. on board as well as a couple of flagons of wine. All in all it was too perfect a day to put into words. After a couple of hours of hot sunshine, a light and welcome breeze stole into the bay and we set sail back across the bay. Back at the marina, the girls left as one had to be taken to the airport. Mike and I finished the wine on the boat and then he bought me dinner in Chinatown. We finished the day in a saloon listening to blue grass.

Tuesday May 29th

Once I got my hangover under control, I made my daily pilgrimage to Safeways then varnished a few dozen cans of food. I bought charts for here to Hawaii and charts for the Delta.

Wednesday May 30th

I finally got my pulpit back together and on the boat. It's been really hot the last few days and my shoulders and back have peeled halfway through to my spine and are now burned all over again. A guy I'd spoken to once before asked me to race with him on Saturday. He has a Santana 20 and there'll just be the two of us. He thinks that because I sailed this far I can teach him something about small boat handling. I went to the yacht club this evening to watch the folkboat races and had dinner there afterwards with Mike and other newer friends. A few of us didn't get out of the bar there until 04:00 and then Mike and I took his boat across the harbour and put her away.

Thursday May 31st

I did a major cleaning and organising today. I cleaned up all of my poor, rusting tools, changed my fresh water and stowed the last batch of provisions. We're pretty well stocked to capacity now and I could probably live off the boat for close to 3 months. Mike stopped by the boat this evening with a lady friend. He has a plumbing problem at his house and he wants me to help him dig a ditch and expose the pipes tomorrow morning. Though I would gladly do it in return for all he has done for me, I know he'll insist on paying me. I'm also going to do a few days work for a friend of his when I get back from the Delta.

Friday June 1st

I dug a hole 5 feet deep in front of Mike's house today. This afternoon, Mike drove me to Alameda to shop for some lines and rigging that I needed. He paid for the rigging and the oysters and beer afterwards in lieu of wages. This evening we had dinner at a Chinese restaurant with eight other people and afterwards drank Watney's Red Barrel at a Scottish-type pub.

Saturday June 2nd

John Hendricks and I raced his Santana 20 today with little success. It was wet and exciting sailing but I like my heavy, slow cruiser better. This evening I loaded everything that has accumulated on the dock back on the boat ready to leave in the morning. Don got me 2 gallons of kerosene for nothing from the gas station that he works at.

Sunday June 3rd

I left the marina at 07:30 and sailed slowly out across the bay with light winds and fog. By the time I reached San Pablo bay, the sun was shining, the wind was blowing briskly from astern and I was having trouble with the helm. It has developed an alarming amount of play. At 14:00 I pulled into Glen Cove Marina and got a berth to check it out. Heeling her over with the topping lift to the next dock, I donned a life jacket and jumped (climbed!) into the water. My worst fears were realised as I discovered that a key holding the rudder to the shaft had corroded away. I'll have to haul her out to repair it. It's my own stupid fault as I put a brass key in a stainless fitting and electrolysis gobbled up the brass. While in the water, I scrubbed the hull. A few people who spotted my Canadian flag came over to chat. One of these, John Walters, has offered me much help. He is going to try and arrange to have me hauled out at a local yard and he is also going to try and find someone locally who can weld stainless steel. I have to phone him at work tomorrow morning. I had a couple of drinks and some good conversation with a couple on the next boat, Bob and Judy. They run the yacht brokerage here and have sailed extensively offshore. Later I was invited to dinner by Bob and Tanam on their 28 foot boat. Bob works for Bob the broker as a salesman and his lovely wife is from Thailand. All in all I've done well since pulling into Glen's Cove.

Monday June 4th

I phoned John Walters this morning from the brokerage office and he has arranged for me to be hauled out tomorrow afternoon in Benicia. The two Bobs were going to Vallejo, a few miles away to bring back a Columbia 45 sail boat and invited me along for the ride. We powered all the way though we did have the genoa up for a while giving us a boost. I spent the afternoon making a sea anchor out of an old sail bag. John stopped by this evening to say that it may be Wednesday before I can get hauled. I spent a couple of hours with Bob and Tanam aboard their boat.

Tuesday June 5th

I spent the entire day sitting in the sun waiting to hear from John. When he came by this evening, it was to say that the haul out was set for high tide at noon tomorrow.

Wednesday June 6th

John came and sailed the 3 miles to the boat yard with me. Old Joe Garske picked up Balandra with his rusty crane and set her on a cradle. I scrubbed her bottom and dismantled the rudder assembly. The brass key was half-eaten away and the skeg had a little play in it.

Thursday June 7th

I epoxied some reinforcing strips to the skeg to beef it up. Joe made a nylon bushing for the shaft and supplied a stainless steel key and I re-assembled the whole unit. My next problem is how to get to Vallejo 10 miles away to get some bottom paint.

Friday June 8th

John came to the rescue once again and drove me to Vallejo. I painted the bottom and was back in the water by 14:00. Bucking an ebb current, I spent 4 hours covering the 10 miles to Honker Bay. Although it is a very exposed anchorage, it was the best that I could reach today. I anchored once then moved further in to get out of the current. As the evening wore on, a breeze picked up blowing directly into the bay. I checked my ranges several times to be sure that the anchor wasn't dragging and at 22:00 went to bed.

Saturday June 9th

The wind continued to increase and a lumpy sea built up. I got up several times to check and everything was secure. At 04:00 there was a bump against the hull and I flew up on deck to find that the anchor had dragged. There was only one other boat in the whole bay and I hit it. That actually was a blessing as there was no damage but it got me on deck before Balandra went on the beach. A guy on the other boat came out and fended me off while I rigged my small danforth and threw it out away from his boat. I hauled up my main anchor and reset it and, by the time I was settled back on both anchors, I was within 2 boat lengths of the shore. I dressed and sat anxiously on deck in the dark with the wind still blowing at 15-20 knots. At 05:00 it was light enough to see and with a little difficulty I sailed out her anchors and got out of there. I had the wind blowing heartily from astern but the current against me which made for a very lumpy and slow ride. It took me about 3 hours to cover the 5 miles to Pittsburg and there I pulled into a small marina, had breakfast and waited for the tide to turn. The tide changed and the wind quit so I motored in the hot sunshine. I stopped off in Antiock for gas and cold beer and by mid-afternoon I was anchored in a narrow slough called Fisherman's Cut.

Sunday June 10th

It's hot and windless again this morning. By 11:00 the temperature inside the boat, with both hatches open, was 90°F. I motored around to Potato slough and found it jammed full of power boats. I found a spot well away from everybody and put down two anchors from the stern and a line from the bow to a tree onshore. The current here is very strong. I tried my hand fishing, with no luck. This area is all flat and featureless and the murky fresh water is uninspiring. It is a wonderland for power boats and water skiers and city folk 'getting away from it all'. I'm sure if I came here with a group of friends I'd have a great time but as it is it tends to accent my loneliness. I'm heading back tomorrow. I'll work for a week or two then get back to sea where there are no other people and therefore no reason to feel lonely. It'll pass, it always does.

Monday June 11th

We got under way at 10:00 and motored along at a good clip, going with the current for a change. When I got out on the San Joaquin River, the wind picked up from dead ahead and I beat into it as far as Antioch where I pulled into a marina for the night. I have had a pain in my gut for several days, just below the breast bone. It's like indigestion but it won't go away. I'm hoping it's just a pulled muscle.

Tuesday June 12th

What a terrible day. The sort of day when I'm tempted to sell my sail boat and take up something safe and easy like mountain climbing or heavyweight boxing! I left Antioch at 07:00 and stopped in Pittsburg at 09:00 to make coffee and check gear oil in the motor. The tide was with me but I had 20 knots of wind in my teeth. I continued under sail as the waves were too steep to motor into. I sailed into Honker Bay over on my ear into where I should have had 4 feet of water, according to the chart. I fetched up abruptly in 2 feet of water. Convinced I was on a localised high spot, I donned life jacket then found I could walk 50 feet from Balandra in any given direction without getting my shirt wet.

I promptly carried the main anchor out astern into armpit-deep water and set the small danforth out abeam. I connected the small anchor to the topping lift to heel her over. I spent the next 3 or 4 hours mostly in the water keeping both lines taught and finally, with the rising tide, I got her into deeper water.

As I hauled the main anchor up, she stuck again and wouldn't come about so I hopped over the side into chest-deep water and turned her. The mainsail was up and I just barely got back aboard as she broke free and sailed away. The tide was now against me, as was the wind and we could make no headway down river so I turned and went back to Pittsburg marina. My hands are stiff and blistered from hauling on lines and there is a bunch of skin missing from my right knee. I've had no rum aboard for a couple of days now and I figure maybe that clouded my judgement. When I got into Pittsburg I went and bought a bottle, as you may have guessed from the handwriting. I figure I earned it!

Wednesday June 13th

I sailed from Pittsburg to Glen Cove Marina this morning, beating into a 15-20 knot wind all of the way. I stayed inside the ship channel most of the time, especially near Honker Bay. I spent the evening with Bob and Tanam.

Thursday June 14th

I left Glen Cove at 08:00 when the tide was just starting to ebb. The wind was blowing briskly in my face and against the current, raising steep and lumpy waves. Halfway across San Pablo Bay, the wind fell light and I shook the reef out of the main and swapped the jib for the jenny. When I got to Angel Island the wind went away and I started the motor. The tide turned against me but, halfway across the bay, a breeze sprang up and with full main and jenny, I held my own and moved sideways across the bay. The wind increased until it was 25 knots or more in the gusts and the tide increased until I was sailing forward but moving rapidly backwards. I had much too much sail up for comfort but I didn't want to stop and reef and change headsails as I knew I'd get pushed so far back that I'd never get in. I started the motor and beat back and forth with it assisting until I finally got inside the breakwater. To my annoyance and consternation,

I found the current in there stronger than ever. It was as if an invisible hand held me back. Finally, defeated, I turned around in disgust and went downwind to Gashouse Cove, a mile away and tied up there for the night.

Overall, I'd say that the last couple of weeks have taught me a very important lesson. Offshore sailing is easier and safer, generally speaking, than coastal or inland sailing. I've also decided, for the second time, that I'll never sail on rivers again in this boat. They are downright hazardous for a boat this size and not much fun to sail on anyway.

Friday June 15th

I motored around to the municipal marina and got a berth for the night. Don came by this afternoon with a large sea bass that Roland had given him and some cold beer. I hacked up the bass and he cooked it on his boat and we proceeded to get very drunk.

Friday June 22nd

I've been working for the past week on Ty Gillespie's house. I've built a closet, a sundeck railing, some stairs, hung a door, plastering etc. Basic stuff for $8 per hour. I have a few more hours to do on Monday and on Tuesday I'll leave for Hawaii. I drove today for the first time in months and Ty has now lent me his Ford van for the weekend. What a treat. I hope I don't get stopped as I don't have a licence. I tried, without success, to get a bulb for my masthead light this week. I finally bought a cheap set of running lights to get me to Hawaii and, in the meantime, I'll have Janie try to get a bulb in British Columbia and mail it to Hilo.

Tuesday June 26th

Today I was to have sailed at dawn for Hawaii. I woke with the alarm at 04:00, after 3 hours sleep. I listened to the wind whistling in the rigging and I listened to the fog horns out on the bay and went back to sleep. At first light (06:00) the wind had moderated but the fog was thick and I decided to forget it and slept until 08:30. I woke then to find Don on my dock laughing and jeering because I hadn't left. Yesterday evening Don gave me a box of goodies for the trip; dried fruit, salted nuts, cookies etc. A Japanese couple on a boat here gave me some canned foods and a Hawaii chart. Some of their cans are from New Zealand as they've just sailed up from there via Tahiti and Hawaii. Mike Webber was down at the boat before I got home yesterday and left a whole, huge salami sausage in the cockpit for me. So many good people, it almost gives me hope for mankind, almost!

I finished the job I'd been doing yesterday and made $250. I now have so much food on board that I can't even change my mind without shuffling food around to make room. I have to step down the pace on spending from now on, I've spent over $600 since I got here 40 days ago and made $250 back. I phoned home yesterday (collect, of course) and spoke to my little brother who is grown up now. When he came on the phone I thought he was my father. I really enjoyed talking to him and can't wait to see him. I phoned Janie (collect, of course) yesterday evening and talked to her for half an hour. It was late and the girls unfortunately were sound asleep. Sitting and thinking now, I know that I'm scared. I wasn't scared before I left British Columbia because I didn't know what to expect. I wasn't scared too much out there because I was out there and had no choice. Here, now, I know what to expect and I'm scared of going out there. I'll do it anyway. I have 25 gallons of fresh water aboard, 3 gallons of kerosene, 2 gallons of cheap and sleazy red wine, half a gallon of cheap and sleazy liquor and a few cans of beer. I also have half a pack of cigarettes for that occasional smoke.

19:30 Thursday June 28th

Well we're back out on the blue Pacific and it's just like the good old days. I crept quietly out of the marina at 07:00

yesterday with the motor already stowed. We slipped across the bay through the early morning fog and a 4 knot ebb tide carried me out under the Golden Gate Bridge. We picked up a fresh westerly breeze and beat into the south west with lots of water coming aboard. Now, I did a fairly good job sealing all of the existing leaks but I'm damned if a dozen new leaks didn't open up to take their place. I now have water trickling in, in spots that never leaked a drop before. Oh well! Resignation!

By mid-afternoon yesterday the wind was a full-blown gale from the north west. I've been at the helm since leaving San Francisco almost continuously (36 hours). She won't self-steer very well as the seas are too big and I only have the storm jib set. The winds have been over 40 knots but she handles fairly well and we've been broad reaching into the south and west (as wind and waves allow). Right now she is hove to with just the storm jib set while I take a break. The sky cleared for the first time this afternoon but I have taken no sights yet. There's lots of time for that. Right now I just want to get south where it's warmer. It's cold here. It's so windy that the white caps in my coffee keep getting in my moustache. I keep telling myself that it can only get better from now on. I've seen several dolphins and a couple of large fish that came to visit when I was hove to earlier. They were round and silver and I swear they had lips. I'll go out and steer again now until well into the night and, if the wind doesn't moderate by then, I'll heave to and sleep until daylight.

12:30 Friday June 29th

I hove to and slept fitfully in my damp bed for a few hours. Heaving to is my new alternative to laying ahull. I set the storm jib on the forestay and sheeted it in tight on the leeward side and lashed the tiller over the same way. She sits nicely and doesn't roll as much. I steered again this morning and when the wind moderated at 09:00, I put up the double-reefed main. The sky was heavily overcast but I could see blue sky to windward, moving rapidly my way. At 11:00 the sky overhead cleared and as it did, so the wind dropped and the seas began to diminish. Within half an hour I had both reefs out of the main, the working jib up and the storm jib steering. Now we're broad reaching briskly over a glittering blue sea and sailing is once again the life for me. I fired up the stove at noon and had a toasted cheese and salami sandwich washed down with rum and coffee. Real sailor's fare! Two or three days should have me down to the north east trade winds and I look forward to that.

14:00 I saw a plane and a freighter at the same time. What a busy world.

19:00 Saturday June 30th

It's blowing 25 knots or so and I'm beam reaching in large seas with double-reefed main and jib. We're moving fast and right on course but it's a wet and bumpy ride. By 16:00 yesterday I was down to this much sail and by nightfall I took in the jib. She ran all night with no problem and I got some sleep. I've had no chance to dry things yet as there is a lot of spray flying. I can't complain as it's a big improvement on the trip down the coast. The temperature in the cabin is 65°F, 15°F better than most of the trip down. The sun has shone for most of the day but I've taken no sights as I know more or less where I am and a little more or less makes no difference at this stage. My primary objective is to get down to the north east trades where it's warmer.

22:00 The wind picked up and I took in the jib at sunset. There is a barely noticeable decrease in speed but the motion is a lot easier. The ocean here is a lot warmer suddenly and the swells are getting funny. At sundown I noticed a lot of dolphins a way off and stood on deck to wait for them. Sure enough they came to play. There were dozens of them, all playing around us, swimming by in formation groups or making bold dashes across our bow. Unfortunately the light was very dim and I could only see them as they broke the surface.

13:30 Sunday July 1ˢᵗ

The wind is still quite strong out of the north west. The seas are large and the sky is mostly clear. I fixed my position at noon and got a pleasant surprise. 255 miles in the past 44 hours! I don't believe it, even allowing for the current giving us half a knot. We're rolling a lot and I figure one of my sights must have been off. I can't believe we could cover that great distance with nothing but the double-reefed main up most of the time.

16:00 The sky is heavily overcast and it looks like rain. The wind is about the same and we're bouncing along under double-reefed main only. I haven't been on deck all day. I appear to have a slight malfunction in my radio – like it doesn't work! I think the dampness got to it so I opened up the back and popped a silica gel bag inside. Bolting the stable door I know, but it might help.

19:15 The weather looks threatening but the barometer is steady and the wind has not increased. The radio is working. Reception is not good now and I think my only problem is poor reception in daylight hours. I'll see if it improves later tonight.

10:00 Monday July 2ⁿᵈ

On AM radio last night I listened to a station in Eugene, Oregon, about 900 miles away. On SW I picked up Radio Australia and (thankfully) the time signal. At 04:00 this morning the wind fell light for a while and it rained. The first rain I've seen in weeks.

20:00 By this afternoon the wind had slowly shifted around until it was due north. I took down the main and rigged the two jibs. The wind right now is very light but we are moving along, headed a little west of south. As we get further south, the wind should move around to the north east and put us right on course. The sky has been overcast all day but now, as the sun sets, it shows signs of clearing.

I took the stove apart this afternoon as it has been misbehaving. I think the plunger for the pump got melted when some burning alcohol spilled under it in rough seas the other day. It's working now but the pump needs new parts. I've done nothing for the past few days but read science fiction books given to me by Henry, National Geographics from Don and Smithsonians from Mike.

14:00 Tuesday July 3rd

I'm just a light breath away from being totally becalmed. Since dawn I've barely maintained steerageway with the twins set, heading due south. The sky has been overcast all day but with so little wind it is pleasantly warm. I washed my hair and body, then festooned the rigging with damp bedding, towels and clothes. I pulled up the floor, mopped out a couple of gallons of water and checked the canned goods. The 6 cans of beer left are corroding badly so I figure today is a good day to dispose of them. I'm starting to realise that I have a ridiculous quantity of food on board. Better too much than not enough, I guess. I should have enough canned food to last me to New Zealand if the cans don't rust first. I had thought that aluminium cans would be OK but I've had 3 coke cans and one beer can corrode right through and spill their contents into the bilge. I also had a chocolate pudding in an aluminium ring pull can pop open and spew its contents over a dozen other cans. Messy! I have the radio on right now and am picking up an AM station from Los Angeles loud and clear.

17:00 We're basically becalmed. There are little breaths of wind now and then but always seemingly from different directions. Balandra is pointed north but, since we're not moving, it doesn't matter. If the Pacific doesn't get specific before dark I'll take the sails down.

10:00 Wednesday July 4th

Just before the sun set yesterday, a light breeze came up out of the west. I took down the jibs and set the jenny and the main. Sailed for 10 minutes and then the wind died again leaving the sails slatting lazily as we rolled on the low swell. At this point I took the sails down and went to bed. This morning the light westerly wind was blowing and we got under way. We're now close reaching into the south west with about 10 knots of wind. The sky is still solidly overcast and I haven't fixed my position for about 3 days now.

14:00 Becalmed again. The sun came out for a while and I fixed my position. We've covered only 125 miles in the past 3 days.

16:00 We're creeping, just barely moving into the south. The wind is out of the west and the sky is still overcast.

19:00 We're moving well into the south west on a light west-nor'-wester. I should be well into the north east trades by now. Twice today I thought I heard engines but on investigation found the horizon clear. The third time I had heard nothing and was but casually glancing about when I spotted a freighter a mile or so off. It was almost like an invasion of my privacy, sneaking up like that. It is most certainly getting warmer. The cabin temperature is about 75° now and I find myself wearing fewer clothes. I drank the last of the rum with my evening coffee, accompanied by my last cigarette. Once again, fully intentional. Even as I write this the wind is failing along with the sun. The sky which had cleared for several hours is once more clouding over.

08:00 Thursday July 5th

The wind held until 01:00 when I was awakened by the loosely flapping sails. A light drizzle was falling as I went on deck and took them down. Soon after I got up this morning the wind came back from the north west with a few small patches of blue peeping through.

18:00 Almost all around the horizon is clear sky but not overhead. The wind held steady but light most of the day as we moved slowly into the south west. We covered 60 miles in the 24 hours to noon today which is pretty good considering the wind. I'm now just north of 30°N on 130°W. Right in the Horse Latitudes. The wind is again failing and we're just maintaining steerageway.

08:00 Friday July 6th

At sunrise the north westerly wind came back and blew briskly for maybe an hour. I'd taken the sails down last night for want of a breeze so this morning I hastened out of bed to set them again. While the wind blew, it rained hard but now the wind has died and the rain is a misty drizzle falling from a leaden sky. Progress has been very slow these last few days but I'll take this any day over laying ahull in a gale.

11:00 Right now the Pacific is like Georgia Strait in August. Mirror smooth with hardly even a swell noticeable. The sun is trying to burn through the low cloud.

17:00 At around noon, a breeze sprang up out of the south!! It blew briskly for maybe an hour but since then we've maintained bare steerageway. In the 24 hours up until noon today we covered only 30 miles. Now, I hate to complain because I've wished so many times recently for the wind to stop, but a little progress would be nice. The only living creatures I see these days are jellyfish. Mostly sailing jellyfish that cover the water like dead leaves in autumn. Their little funny sails up, drifting with the breeze. I haven't seen a bird in days. I'm over 500 miles from land but that wouldn't bother my friend the albatross.

08:00 Saturday July 7th

The wind died yet again yesterday evening and I took the sails down for the night. When I woke this morning there was a breeze blowing from the north, north west. I lost no time setting the twins. By the time I had everything rigged, the wind was out of the east. I had to unrig the twins and get the main up. By the time the main was up, the wind was out of the south and I quit and came below for coffee and breakfast. Now there is no wind at all and the lifeless mainsail is flopping monotonously back and forth as we roll on the glassy swells.

13:00 We have wind, real wind, complete with waves. Unfortunately it's out of the south east so we're beating once again. The pilot chart says you don't get south easterly winds here so maybe I should just ignore it. Where oh where are the north east trades.

13:20 The wind just died right away.

20:30 The wind returned but still from the south east. It's brisk enough to have us moving well, right on course. I hope it holds until morning, I just hate getting up and messing with sails in the dark. Today has been overcast and cool, not at all tropical and I spent most of the day below reading old magazines. I haven't started a single letter yet but I guess I'll have plenty of time for such diversions, after all I've only been at sea for 11 days.

08:00 Sunday July 8th

The wind held all night and increased until we were over on our ear, pounding through the white caps. I did not sleep as I was sure of a change. At dawn I found things unchanged under a heavily overcast sky. I was ready to put a reef in the main a few minutes ago but the wind now seems to be moderating.

17:00 I put that reef in the main this morning and we've spent all day over on our ear pounding through 4 to 6 foot seas. The sky has cleared and it's typical trade winds weather except the wind is from entirely the wrong direction. Everything is starting to get wet again from the waves washing over but at least it's warm. A jet just flew overhead on a reciprocal course to mine. I've heard of people sailing to Hawaii using jet streams as their only means of navigation.

21:30 I've taken down the jib so that I can get some rest tonight. Pounding to windward gets awfully tiring after a couple of days. We're now moving more slowly and a little more westerly under mainsail and steering sail and the motion is much easier. Almost peaceful in fact.

08:00 Monday July 9th

I guess the ocean figured I was still making good progress with a south wind. This morning I find it still blowing briskly but out of the south west, right where I have to go. Ask anyone about sailing from California to Hawaii in July and they tell you it's a sleigh ride. Best month of the year, north east trades blow gently and constantly once you clear the coast. Racing boats do the trip in 14 days, cruisers taking it easy take 21 days. This is my 13th day at sea and I'm about one third of the way there. Maybe it's something I said.

19:30 The wind is still out of the south west and the best course I can make is a little north of west. It's been overcast and cool all day and now a light drizzle is falling. Other than putting the jib back up this morning, I haven't been on deck all day.

09:30 Tuesday July 10th

Last night at 22:00 the wind died right away and I took down the sails. This morning we are almost becalmed but a few tiny breaths of air are rippling the surface portending wind to come (I hope). I swear what wind there is, is from the north east unless it's my overly taxed imagination. Mustering what little optimism I have left, I rigged the twins. Right now a light rain is falling and the sails are flopping loosely as we roll on yesterday's leftover swells.

16:00 What little breeze there is, is out of the east and I'm moving very slowly westward. I've left the twins up as I'm sure that when the wind picks up it will back towards the north. (Please!). It has been fairly warm and sunny all day so I closed the seacock on the cockpit drain, filled the cockpit with sea water and took a bath. It's awfully nice to be clean (I was starting to smell so bad).

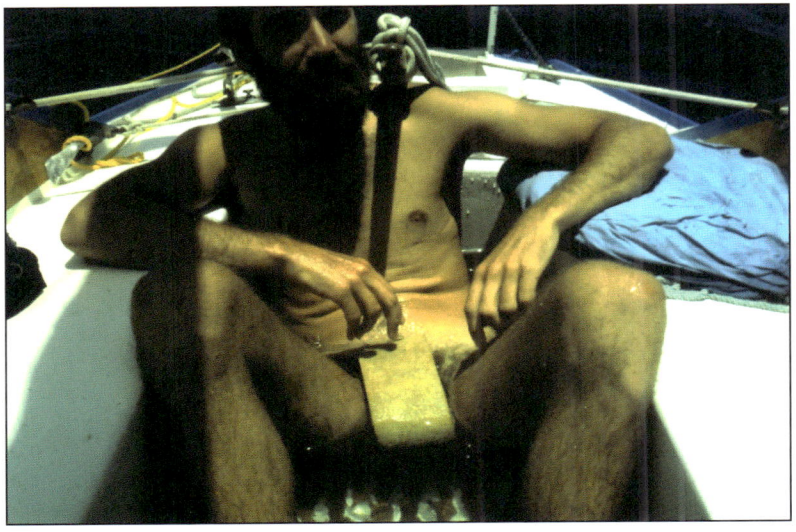

21:00 Other than what the current has given me, I doubt that I've covered more than 10 miles in the last 24 hours. The wind is still very, very light. At times not even enough for steerageway. I had a hot sponge pudding with chocolate sauce out of a can for supper. It had been given to me by a Japanese couple in San Francisco and they had carried it all the way from New Zealand.

11:00 Wednesday July 11th

Still no wind. Dawn revealed low clouds, rain and limp sails so I lay in bed until late, reading and drinking coffee. I'm going to run out of priming alcohol for the stove before I reach Hawaii. I was sure that I had another quart of it but that cannot now be found. I also forgot to buy spare tanks for my little propane stove and I used the last of the propane when beating to windward. I now ration myself to lighting the stove once a day.

12:00 We have wind! Not much but enough to keep the sails asleep and it's out of the north east.

15:00 My God, I think we've found it. The fabled and elusive north east trade wind. It's still raining and visibility is less than half a mile (not much to see out here anyway). The wind is about 15 knots and we're bouncing along dead downwind, right on course. Hawaii here we come. We still have about 1,200 miles to go so we'll be close to another 2 weeks at sea yet.

19:00 The rain has finally stopped and a few patches of blue are peeping through the clouds. The wind is a little lighter now but quite adequate and still out of the north east. I spent my time closed up in the cabin today making myself a serviceable and, I think, good looking hat.

09:00 Thursday July 12th

It's raining again but the wind is good. During the night the wind fell away to almost nothing. Several times she slowly rounded up and stalled and I had to get up each time and put her back on course. I was rewarded for my efforts by a brilliant full moon, reflecting across the still water. With the early morning rain, the wind returned.

17:00 The rain stopped at about noon but it's still overcast. The wind has held steady east, north east at 10-15 knots. As of today I've covered 800 miles and have about 1,150 to go.

09:00 Friday 13th July

A freighter just crossed my stern, close enough for me to make out the name 'Eastern Grace' through the binoculars. It's the first sign of life I've seen in a while. The wind is still fair and the sky overcast with a few patches of blue.

20:30 The wind has freshened somewhat and we're going like a train. The sun has shone on and off for most of the day and it has been most pleasant. I dug out some of my home-dried peaches and plums today but found some of them infested with little critter eggs. I'll not throw them out, I'll just eat them in the dark. Speaking of 'little critters', I found a dead, 3 inch long squid on deck this morning. I have a pain in my chest that has been growing for 3 days now. It's in the region of my surgery but is a good deal more severe than my normal pain. It's certainly not incapacitating, just very uncomfortable.

10:00 Saturday July 14th

The sky is overcast this morning and it is fairly cool. The wind is fresh and steady and we're flying into the south west. I found my first ever flying fish in the cockpit this morning but I didn't have it for breakfast. It was only 3 inches long and I don't know how it cleared even our freeboard.

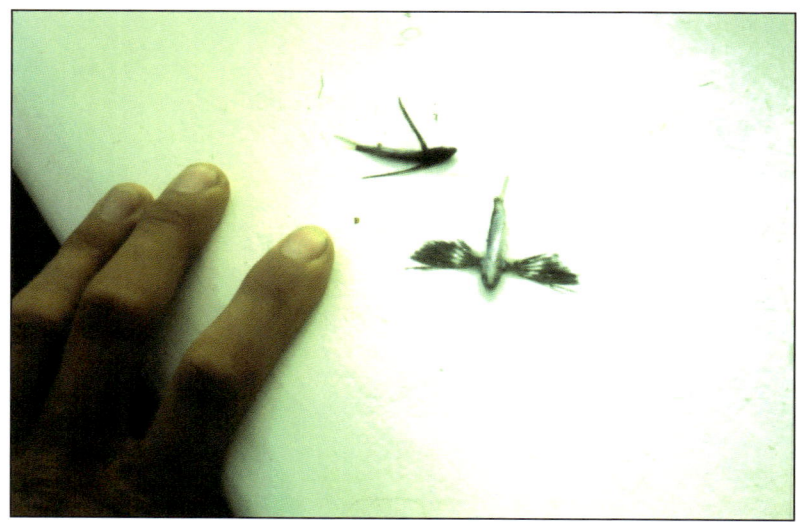

13:00 We seem to be making very slow progress considering the wind we have and the current that should be giving us 12 miles a day. We've covered 90 miles in the last 24 hours and 90 in the 24 hours before. We're exactly halfway so it's downhill from here on.

20:00 I remembered this afternoon that 135°W is a time zone. Accordingly I set my watch back 1 hour. I never wear a watch but keep it strapped to a boat frame. It's use is mainly limited to the hours of darkness when I might want to know how long until daylight. I can tell how long until nightfall by the sun. My quartz crystal watch is kept set on GMT. It has been mostly sunny today and I got a little burned on the parts of my anatomy not exposed for tanning in civilised lands. The wind is still good and the sky again overcast.

09:00 Sunday July 15th

The wind is quite strong this morning and the sky mainly overcast. Running dead downwind like this with no fore and aft sails set, the rolling motion is lively to say the least. The seas have built up over the past few days and at times, threaten to overpower the rudder. If she takes the waves square in, there is no problem, in fact we get a boost as we surf on them. But, if a large wave catches her to one side it slews the stern around. Twice in the night we were turned forcefully, broadside on to the wind where we stall. I then have to go out and haul on sheets until she falls off and starts running again. I have slept little in the last few days on account of the motion. The pain in my chest is still quite severe.

18:30 The seas are ridiculously large for the amount of wind there is and the motion is, at times, quite violent. The sky has been overcast all day, which is as well as it has allowed my burned portions to cool off. I spent part of today sorting, numbering and describing slides, ready to sendl home. I saw a freighter to the west at 16:30.

07:30 Monday July 16th

I feel better this morning than I have felt for a while. I got some sleep last night by laying athwartships, with my upper body reclining against the port cabinets and my feet upon the starboard quarter berth. It wasn't really comfortable but it sure beat getting rolled from one side of my berth to the other all night. The seas have gone down just a little this morning and the day welcomed me with a double rainbow. The sky is mostly overcast still and it rained during the night. I found a small squid and a tiny flying fish on deck.

08:00 Tuesday July 17th

The pain in my chest is worse again today but now I know why. It's the singing. I like to sing and at sea, I sing at great volume. I spent an hour on deck yesterday singing lustily and in the evening noticed that the pain was worse. I also seem to recall having a good sing just prior to it getting bad a few days ago. Hell of a thing when a guy can't even sing any more. Oh well, maybe now I'll see more marine life! The wind this morning is a little brisker once again and the seas have built up since yesterday. It's still overcast with some sunny spells and some showers. Life gets pretty boring out here. I grow tired of sitting and reading but there is little else to do. I haven't touched the helm or the sails for 5 days now. I spend 15 minutes a day fixing my position and maybe another 15 looking over fittings and lines for signs of wear. There are really only the two jib sheets in use and I keep them well waxed where they pass through the block. The constant motion precludes doing anything constructive and the only time I can pick up anything on the radio is after dark. As the old saying goes, 'Sometimes I sits and thinks and sometimes I just sits'!! I've not yet run out of reading materials fortunately.

15:00 Well, we covered 115 miles in the 24 hours up until noon today. That now leaves 675 miles to go. The wind shifted a little easterly today and I had to adjust sails and helm to keep us on course. The sky is still mainly overcast. I'll still be so pale when I reach Hawaii, nobody will believe I've been at sea for a month.

07:30 Wednesday July 18th

What a beautiful morning. The sun rose in unsurpassable splendour of gold and blue to illuminate a world of clear skies and little waves. Unfortunately there are clouds appearing over the horizon already.

I slept poorly last night. The wind blew very hard for a while then shifted to the east and fell light. I adjusted the sails accordingly but with the wind so light and the seas so large we were flipped sideways on to the wind several times and stalled. Each time I'd have to stand up in the hatch and haul on the windward sheet until she fell off. The wind is now out of the north east but lighter than it has been.

10:00 The wind just shifted to the east and fell very light. Dark clouds are moving in and it looks like it may rain.

13:00 Well the beautiful start didn't last very long. Since 10:00 it has been overcast and raining with light contrary winds. The wind is presently out of the east and we have bare steerageway. In the last 24 hours we covered only 80 miles.

16:00 A most frustrating day. The wind shifted right around to the south east and, with the twins set, I could do no better than west, north west even by sitting at the helm. I was loathe to take them down but as the wind from the south east freshened, it seemed like the only thing to do. I left them rigged but just dropped the whole mess on deck then hoisted the main. We're now moving slowly south west with just main and steering sail set and it is raining once more.

18:30 After eating dinner I decided I'd better set the jenny to get some speed. I hoisted it without unhanking the jibs, which worked OK. Within 30 minutes I noticed a large dark cloud mass moving toward us from the north east although the wind was still from the south east. I dropped the main and jenny and was just getting the twins organised when the north east wind hit us along with a torrential but short-lived downpour. It didn't take long for me to be soaked to the skin as that was all I was I was wearing. It washed off the salt from this afternoon's bath anyway. So the trade winds are back, though still a little light.

21:00 The wind has again shifted and fallen very light. It's now a little south of east and I'm just able to hold a westerly course with the twins set.

08:00 Thursday July 19th

The trades came back with a bang at 03:00 and have been blowing briskly since then, keeping us right on course.

13:30 We have 525 miles to go as of noon. We've made too much westing and we're a good deal north of where we want to be. The sky has been clear for several hours now and I've been sprawled naked in the cockpit soaking up the sun. I think I'm now cooked enough for today. I cleaned out the bilge and had to throw out a couple of cans of chocolate pudding that had started to seep.

21:00 Well today has certainly been the nicest yet and the closest to what people picture as ideal cruising. After a beautiful golden sunset, the stars appeared one by one in the clear sky to be rivalled only by the constant glittering phosphorescence that accompanies us every night. There will be a tiny sliver of moon tonight but not until very late.

10:00 Friday July 20th

Now, this is tropical. I slept last night with the main hatch open and a million or 3 stars peeping in. The sky this morning is mostly clear and it's already hot. 80°F in the cabin. The wind is a little lighter than I'd like but we're moving along alright. If this pain in my chest would just quit, life would be perfect.

15:15 I have another sailboat in sight. He's right astern and seems to be on the same course so he should overtake me in a few hours. After all, everybody is faster than Balandra. This is exciting. As of noon we were about 400 miles from Hawaii. The sun has been shining all day so this morning I built a sun deck. I put a piece of plywood over the cockpit well, covered that with the rug and spread some foam. It gives me a flat area about 4 feet by 6 feet on which to sit and lay comfortably. I hope that other boat comes over to talk.

20:00 Well I had no visitors. He passed across my stern about 3 miles away and vanished over the western horizon. I spent all day naked in the sun and now my skin is tight and just a trifle tender in places.

09:30 Saturday July 21st

It looks like another hot and sunny day coming up. I should keep my bum covered today, it's a little tender.

17:30 Well the hot, sunny day turned out to be overcast and showery. I wrote to Rick today for the first time in many months. I also wrote a letter to mum and dad and sealed it in an envelope to be opened in the event of my death. A sort of will and goodbye letter. My chest obviously has me worried. We now have a little over 300 miles to go. I'll be awfully glad to get there. We crossed another time zone today and I put my watch back an hour.

20:00 The wind has increased in the last couple of hours and the sea is now running quite high. We're still well north of where we need to be but can't get any further to the south with the twins steering. Tomorrow morning I'll strike the twins and rig the main and jenny and head south, south west.

08:30 Sunday July 22nd

It was very lumpy all night and I got little sleep. I took down the twins at first light and just as I was putting up the main, a squall struck with winds over 30 knots and pouring rain. It only lasted about an hour and now we have gentler winds and clearer skies. She won't self-steer on the course I want to sail so I'm going to steer all day and see how we are doing this evening. My chest hurts like hell and I have a numbness through my shoulder and down my left arm. I'm sure it's in the muscle as my breathing seems OK.

15:00 What was it Popeye used to say, 'I've had all I can stands and I can't stands no more'. I've been at the helm all day but now she is left to her own devices with just the double-reefed main set. The winds have been strong and gusty all day with very large seas. The wind has moved more northerly so there are new swells superimposed on the old to confuse the seas more. I've been alternately soaked then dried by the sun and wind so many times that my whole body is caked with gritty salt. If the wind were to go down a little I could probably steer my course now with the twins set again. 220 miles to go as of noon. With good conditions I could be there the day after tomorrow. We'll see.

18:00 Well I guess I could stand a little more as I went right back on the helm. The wind is very strong and the seas are the largest we've had since leaving San Francisco. I've been steering all afternoon with just the double-reefed main but right now she's ahull while I rest and eat. I can't bring myself to just sit all night when we're so close so I'm going back on the helm and steer for as much of the night as I can handle. I'll try her with just the jib.

07:00 Monday July 23rd

I hung in there until midnight at the helm, tired and soaked through and through. Then I left her with the storm jib up and came below for some sleep. This morning it is still blowing the same so I'll go out and steer after I've had something to eat. Yesterday afternoon, while below eating, I was thrown off balance by a wave and struck my right shoulder hard. Now it's bruised and painful and my right hand and wrist are sore from steering. The pain in my chest seems to have loosened up a little with the exercise.

14:00 Conditions have now moderated and she is steering herself with the twins set. We're steering as close to the course needed as we can but we're still a little north. I'll take some sights this afternoon and get an update. Hawaii should be within 150 miles by now. My body is very tired. Sitting at the helm of a small boat in big seas is hard work. I just tried the radio and can pick up an AM station in Honolulu faintly.

17:00 130 miles to go as of right now to Hilo, my first port. We're moving well right now and pretty well on course. With these conditions holding and a little bit of luck, I could have my feet on dry land by tomorrow evening. With clear skies I should be able to see land tomorrow morning. Mauna Kea and Mauna Loa are awfully big mountains, each almost two and a half miles high. I can't stop thinking about how nice it is going to be to be tied up to the land again.

07:30 Tuesday July 24th

I've been up since first light at 06:00, looking for the mountains. There's too much low cloud on the horizon to see anything just yet. The sky overhead is clear now as it is to windward so maybe in an hour or so??? I've taken a sight and got one line of position but that doesn't tell me much until I can cross it with another in a couple of hours.

11:30 We're quite a bit to the north of where we want to be and still 70 miles distant from Hilo. So we won't be there today as I won't approach the land in the dark. Right now we're close reaching due south and what I have in mind is to hold this course until we're dead to windward of Hilo, at which time we should be about 30 miles offshore. Then we'll heave to until morning and run right in. The horizon is still clouded right in and I can see nothing to confirm my position. It's times like this that I worry about my navigation skills (or lack of them!). I'm picking up a Hilo radio station now and it's signal is stronger than it was last night so I live in hope.

16:30 The wind is very light and we're moving slowly. We may end up sailing all night at this speed. Hilo is still over 50 miles away. No sleep for me tonight.

20:30 Well I guess I found it. I have lights all across the south west horizon with a flashing light to the south. There is sky glow of a town that has to be Hilo and I'm pretty sure the flashing light is Cape Kunnukahi, the easternmost point of the island. The bearings on the sky glow and the light put me about 40 miles out but it doesn't look that far so I'm playing it safe. We're laying ahull and I'll get under way again a couple of hours before daylight. The lights I can see would have to be well up in the hills for me to see them from 40 miles off. We'll see. The wind is still fairly light which suits me for tonight.

02:00 Wednesday July 25th

It's a black night with not even a star to light my way. There are three distinct patches of sky glow and we're headed for the centre one, running before a light breeze with Gemini steering. It should start to get light around 05:30 or so.

03:30 I chickened out. I'm sure that is Hilo and I can see the street lights distinctly but no navigational lights. That is, there are some red flashing lights but the ones I need to see should be white or green. I'm sure I'm still miles offshore but it's hard to judge exactly so I figure, for the sake of a couple of hours, I'll wait. For all I really know, I could have the wrong island entirely.

08:00 When the sky turned grey at 05:00 I got the sails up and headed in. Now the sun is up I can see a lot less. The horizon is solid cloud and rain and I can only make out indistinct blotches of land in a couple of places. I seem to be still about 15 maybe 20 miles off but it's hard to say for sure. I got a bearing on the lights before they vanished so I'll head in and see what's what.

14:30 Well I got in and got the hook down in Radio Bay, Hilo at about 11:00 and I'm now well on my way to a good drink. There are about a dozen boats in here, all with an anchor off the stern (wrong end!) and their bows up to the sea wall. People were most impressed when I got settled using only sails. The motor is still stowed under the cockpit. I got cleared and went to the store and bought 6 beers, a bottle of vodka, a quart of milk and 2 mangoes. The first 3 days are free but if you stay longer then you are charged $3 a day from day one. I'll stay 3 days. I spent the evening on other people's boats, chatting and telling and being told sea stories. Victor Shane sailed his 20 foot trimaran here from Santa Barbara, California. Another guy, Terrell Pool, sailed 'Stride' which is about 24 feet overall.

Thursday July 26th

Vic has rented a car for a few days and today he took Terrell and me into town. We all went grocery shopping at Safeway to restock. I spent $72. I then tripped around town and had lunch at Macdonald's. I stowed everything and phoned Janie this evening. Afterwards, I spent a couple of hours aboard 'Big Bear' a 45 foot 'down Easter' schooner owned by Helmut and Anne. Sadly this boat was consequently lost on Christmas Island some years later.

17:00 Friday July 27th

Vic loaned me his bicycle today and I went into town (about 4 miles). It's the first time I've ridden a bike since I was 16. I bought charts of the Hawaiian islands and managed to find some stove alcohol and a new kerosene lamp. Back at the boat, the afternoon showers started and I stayed below writing. Tomorrow I leave for Maui and I know that some people are waiting to see how I make out sailing off my anchor alone in this tight spot. I hope the wind is light and I don't screw it up.

12:00 Saturday July 28th

Well, after 3 days ashore here I am out on old Mr. Ocean again. We're presently becalmed about 3 to 4 miles from shore and it's taken me 2 hours to get this far. I left the motor stowed, took up the anchor in a flat calm and had to paddle a few yards to pick up a breeze and ghost out of there. I saw a four and a half foot shark a little while ago and tried to ram him but he was too quick. We've had a couple of heavy showers already. Before I left I had breakfast aboard Big Bear with Helmut and Anne.

19:00 We picked up a breeze out of the east at 15:00. Pleasant sailing in the sunshine. I had a couple of drinks and then, at about 17:00, she started to blow. Nothing sobers you up like reefing the mainsail in a lumpy sea. We're now on a fast beam reach headed north and it's a wet and bumpy ride. It's getting dark now but no sleep for me tonight.

11:00 Sunday July 29th

By 22:00 last night I had a second reef in the main and we were still flying. By 02:00 I figured we had gone far enough north but not wishing to struggle with the twins in the dark, I let her jog along under just double-reefed main until daylight. I had an hour or two's sleep in brief naps. I had the twins up by 05:30 and since then, we have been having a pleasant run west, south west in the sunshine. The wind and seas had moderated by this morning and now the wind is getting a little too light. After being becalmed yesterday, I knew I couldn't make Kahului Harbour in 24 hours so I deliberately went well offshore and will spend today running back in. I will probably heave to for a few hours overnight then get there tomorrow in daylight. I have my fishing line rigged with my new Mahi Mahi lure but no bites yet. Last night, while double-reefing the main, I slipped on the wet deck and came very close to falling overboard although naturally I was hooked on with my safety harness.

16:40 Land ho! I have the southern tip of Maui in sight though still a long way off. Today has been most pleasant sailing. The wind has been right astern, blowing a comfortable 10 to 12 knots and we've been in no hurry as we'll have to stop for a while later anyway. After absorbing sufficient sunshine earlier, I retired below to several drinks and a good book. It's by a guy who sailed a 25 foot boat across an ocean all alone, if you believe that. Actually, all sarcasm aside, it's a good book and I can relate better than most to what he is saying. You read all of this guff about single-handing, the hardships, loneliness, suffering, anxiety, stress, boredom and by God, it's all true. But isn't it nice when people look at your boat in awe and say "you really sailed that from the mainland alone?" People photograph her (and me) constantly and, shaking me by the hand, congratulate me on a great achievement. It almost makes it worthwhile to stick it out a little longer. I have to keep moving though. I cannot actually afford to 'cruise' the South Sea Islands, just pass through them. I'll take a sun sight now and cross it with a bearing on the land, then it's supper time.

18:30 I just hooked into a fish but it got away. I could see it thrashing on the surface as I tried to bring it in and it was for sure, the biggest fish I've ever hooked. Maybe next time I'll land him. I now know exactly where I am and I'm going to hold this course, have a couple of drinks then, at midnight I'll take down the sails and sleep for a few hours. I hope I get a fish before the sun goes down.

20:00 What a day! I found a green and white flashing light on the horizon that's not on my chart and whilst I was checking and pondering this, a sea monster took my line. The trip line (tied to a tin mug) tugged and snapped, the heavy shock cord (to snub the fish's momentum) stretched to capacity and then the braided Dacron line with a breaking strength of 250 pounds snapped like string. I retained most of the line but lost the lure and steel leader. After that I picked up a 15 second flashing light on the horizon right where it was supposed to be. We lay ahull for the rest of the night in a steep, choppy sea and fresh breeze.

10:00 Monday July 30th

Kahului harbour hasn't impressed me much yet. The wind blows right in here though the swells are stopped by the breakwater. The bottom is coral and I put down the 20 pound fisherman for the first time ever. It seems to be holding OK but I get very anxious when it blows like this. I have to get out the dinghy to get ashore (another first) then, on shore, there is no secure place to stow it. We'll just hope that the "Aloha" spirit is alive and well and living on Maui. There appears to be hotels all along the beach so I hope they're not private beaches.

10:30 An afterthought, I'm not sure I can row that inflatable dinghy in this much wind. I've never ever even had it in the water. I can get ashore easily, fast too but getting back??? I'm thinking I should practice rowing to windward by setting out another anchor. I've never felt the need to do that before but I think it would be the 'seamanlike' thing to do. It's blowing a good 25 knots and more in the gusts. So far we haven't dragged an inch.

15:30 It's still blowing and I haven't unstowed the dinghy yet. It's been blowing really hard and gusty so I put a kellet down the anchor line. I have the other anchor set to go if I need it. A ray of some kind swam by on the surface not 8 feet away, slowly flapping his 4 foot wing span. There is not one other cruising boat in the bay so I guess Kahului doesn't have much to offer. I might head for Lahaina first thing tomorrow. It's a resort area and is on the leeward side of Maui. I'll have good weather but very light winds there. I feel the need to just stay somewhere for a little while and collect myself but Hilo cost money and this spot is too breezy. Lahaina is about 30 miles away, a nice day sail.

18:30 I do not like this anchorage. The wind has shifted now to due north and is blowing right through the opening in the breakwater. I've yet to have a real north wind out on the ocean, the trades are predominantly easterly. I'd be happier outside with sails up right now, I feel so vulnerable in here. The rocky beach is 200 yards to leeward. I have the danforth set under foot with the 100 feet rode free to run so that I have a warning system. I went ashore for a couple of hours and bought a few groceries. Not much of a town. I'd like to leave in the early morning but I must get some sleep. If it does pick up and blow, I won't sleep too well. Last night my sleep was disturbed by a vessel that came and hove too around midnight, not 1 mile from where I lay. Dawn revealed what I took for a small freighter. It turned out to be a Japanese tuna fishing boat. Huge for a fishing boat! I got under way first with dawn's first glimmer but he passed me and is now at a pier about a quarter of a mile away. Rowing back to Balandra in the dinghy against the wind reminded me of Tsawwassen where I kept her last summer. I got very wet!

10:30 Tuesday July 31st

Gemini is once more steering on a broad reach with the north coast of Maui slipping by, a mile off our port beam. Molokai is dead ahead and soon we'll steer a little to port and pass between the two islands. The wind picked up at 08:00 this morning, just in time to give me a few anxious moments sailing out the anchor but everything went smoothly.

17:30 I am so tired! Physically drained. I'm anchored in the lee of Mala wharf about 1 mile from Lahaina, right where I want to be. After the beat out of Kahalui bay, we had a nice run with the trades blowing gently but firmly. As we got into the Pailolo channel, the wind picked up and we were romping but it wasn't that which tired me. Half way through the channel, I had to strike the twins and change course with jib and reefed main. Now I was steering on a wild, fast, rollercoaster beam reach but that didn't tire me. Then we ran into the land shadow and spent 3 hours covering the last 2 miles under a blazing sun. That tired me. There was a very light chop but no swells. Wow! The wind would die away to nothing, sails hanging limp. Suddenly a dark line appears astern moving rapidly towards us. I push out the boom and start the jib sheet as it hits and bang, it's blowing 15 to 20 knots and we fly like a thoroughbred over the ruffled sea. Then suddenly the sails are flogging and the wind has shifted 180° without pause or warning. I tighten in the sheets on the preferred tack and we're over on our ear, spray flying as we slice through the small waves that, as suddenly again give way to glassy ocean and flat calm. The sails slat noisily and I sheet them in tight and keep looking around for the next squall. I'm anchored in about 30 feet of water with a kellet on the danforth. I figure I'm covered now as the bottom is coral and sand. I may stay here for a few days and relax. I haven't really had a chance to do that since San Francisco. I'm going to clean up now and then go ashore and see what Polynesian delights I can find.

Wednesday August 1st

I spent yesterday evening in a bar drinking COLD beer and rowed home around midnight. That inflatable dinghy is a real pig to row, especially in a breeze. This morning a guy named John rowed over and had coffee with me. He has a 20 foot sailboat and is just learning to sail. He and a friend and I took his boat out this morning so he could get my opinion of her and a sailing lesson. I taught him a few things but lack of wind and self-confidence on his part forestalled any serious educating.

I rowed ashore late afternoon and walked into Lahaina (about 1 mile). It was too late in the day to call customs (again). I had dinner at Macdonalds then slipped into a bar for one quick beer. Well maybe two. Then two pretty ladies came and sat beside me so I ordered a third. In conversation, it transpired that they were on a five day holiday from Oahu. They worked there and had an apartment near Waikiki beach. It was so nice to talk to ladies, especially attractive and intelligent ones. They bought a bottle of champagne and shared it with me and I borrowed a knife from the barman and showed them how to cut up and eat a mango in a civilised (though still somewhat messy) manner. The good-natured barman wiped up the pool of mango juice on the bar with a smile and took back his sticky knife. Then he bought me a drink. The girls, Judy and Pam had to fly back to Oahu this evening and left me sitting in the bar but they wrote down their address and insisted that I visit them when I get to Honolulu. Sounds promising.

Thursday August 2nd

It is 10:00 and so far I've only just managed breakfast. I really must phone customs this morning.

Later: I phoned customs, found a fishing store and bought a new mahi mahi lure ($8 this time, I was shocked, but the lady had already rigged it for me). I went back to the boat in the early afternoon and rigged the spinnaker as an awning. I did some serious drinking and by nightfall, when I had planned to go into town, I was ready for bed.

Friday August 3rd

I mailed slides home and walked all around town. Back at the boat I spent the afternoon sewing and reinforcing head sails.

It's the weekend so I'll get dressed up and go to the bar this evening.

Saturday August 4th

That is it. No more hanging around bars. I don't know why I torment myself. I don't mean the hangover either, although it is real enough. I spent the whole evening watching beautiful girls come and go and I didn't speak to a single one. I drank so much that when it was time to go home, no matter how much I tried, I couldn't maintain a straight line. I was pretty disgusted with myself.

14:00 Being in a very depressed state this morning, I decided to sail to Kaanapali where I had to go to buy a chart of Lanai. Sailing my boat is one thing that I do reasonably well and I decided it would boost my morale to sail her. I got the anchor up in very, very light, southerly winds with full main and jenny set. Ghosting along, we made about 2 miles when, with little warning, the wind struck from the north and knocked us flat. Suddenly it was blowing close to 30 knots and as I struggled to get the sails down, I heard the dinghy flopping about at the end of its line. By the time Balandra was under control, the oars were gone. I double reefed the main and searched as best I could but it was blowing ferociously and, even with two reefs in the main, she was hard to handle. We ran off before the wind and as suddenly as it started, it stopped as we passed a certain point and left us slatting about in a flat calm. I shook out the reefs and reset the jenny and in light southerly airs, made my way despondently back to the anchorage at Maha. So much for my morale boost. I'm now going ashore to buy a bottle of rum. I'll paddle in with a 5 foot, 1 by 4 board that has been cluttering up the port quarter berth for months. I knew it would come in handy one day.

19:00 Soon after I last wrote, the wind picked up and was soon blowing a solid 30 knots with gust up to 40 knots. I grew apprehensive of the holding power of my two anchors in the coarse sand and rock before such an onslaught. They dragged. As soon as I was aware that we were dragging (and I was watching), I took off the sail cover and tied two reefs in the main. I got the kellet on board followed by the danforth. By this time we had dragged to within 8 feet of the end of the pier but were passing by it. I got the fisherman anchor on board quickly (it was dragging freely) with the anchor lines in a tangled mess on the foredeck. By now we were on the far side of the pier and the current was carrying us in along it. I hoisted the scrap of mainsail and she promptly rounded up and headed for the pilings. I did the mad 20 foot sprint forward and fended off with no more than a scratch or two on the pulpit. Now clear of danger, I let her jog along practically hove to with the main sheeted in tight while I tidied ship and formulated a plan of action. It was blowing too hard to get to weather and back behind the pier and I didn't care much for that prospect anyway. Finally, I hoisted the little orange storm jib, dropped the main and ran off before the wind towards Lahaina. I'm now anchored in 30 feet of water just off Lahaina boat basin (it's full), (always). Two anchors down again and they seem to be holding. It's still blowing hard and I can't see me getting ashore for that bottle of rum today. I don't like it here. If I'd had the chart for Lanai I would have headed over there this afternoon, it's only 15 miles. The wind is still howling. I don't like this. I'm going to have another glass of cheap and sleazy red wine to calm my nerves.

10:00 Sunday August 5th

The wind fell off last night and I slept from 21:00 through to 07:00. This morning the wind is again blowing hard out of the north but the anchors are holding. I badly need to get ashore but even with oars it would be a struggle rowing against this wind. I'm afraid to leave here without at least a look at a Lanai chart and I still want that bottle. If someone passes close by with an outboard on their dinghy I may try and hitch a tow ashore.

19:00 Things have improved slightly. I got a tow ashore from a small power boat and did a little shopping. I had lunch at Macdonalds then hung around the dinghy dock waiting for a tow back to Balandra. I had decided that I needed more chain for anchoring in coral and if the marine supply store had been open today, I probably would have bought it. Then I met a guy named John at the dinghy dock and it came up, quite by chance, that he had some chain that he wanted to sell. He is a diver and had found it on the bottom along with an anchor. I got a tow to Balandra then John bought the chain over. I gave him $10 for about 22 feet of chain, a good deal for me and a freebie for him. I also have an invitation for dinner aboard his boat (a trimaran) in about an hour's time. Also, whilst ashore, I talked to some people on a 26 foot sail boat from Honolulu who gave me some information on that port. They also gave me a look at a Lanai chart and a large pineapple, not to mention a cold beer.

08:00 Monday August 6th

By 22:00 last night there were no lights showing on John's boat so I guess he got tied up ashore. I was disappointed as he had promised me some fish and magazines in exchange for a book I gave him. Oh well. This morning I sail for Manele Bay on the south side of Lanai (about 15 miles). It's flat calm right now and I think I'll pull out the seagull. Apparently I'll need it to get into Manele anyway and I will surely need it in Honolulu. It's been stowed under the cockpit for a month and a half so I hope it'll run OK.

19:00 I got the two anchors up with difficulty – the fisherman bought up about 20 pounds of coral with it. The seagull started on the second pull and impressed me greatly. I motored for about four hours over glassy seas trailing my new lure but with no luck. 15:00 saw me tied up to a dock in Manele bay, behind the breakwater. It's nice not to have to worry about anchors and dinghies. There are a dozen or so sail boats in here but I'm the only non-American. Usually people see the flag and come over to talk but here no one has so much as said hello, except for one little kid. I had my first hot shower since San Francisco this afternoon. The funny thing is that there is no cold water, only hot. I was so hot and sticky today I would have preferred an ice cold shower.

Tuesday August 7th

I scrubbed the bilges and the deck this morning. Some cans are pretty rusty but most are holding out OK. I aired all of the bedding then rigged an awning and relaxed with a book. A young lad of 14, here on a sail boat with his family from Honolulu, came over to chat. He and his family are all born-again Christians and he spent some time explaining that to me. As we talked, a sail boat came in and it transpired that I was in his berth so I pulled out, set an anchor off the stern and tied the bow to the end of the dock. My young friend Andy came back after dinner and stayed on my boat until 23:00. I enjoyed his company.

Wednesday August 8th

A San Franciscan boat came in to the bay this morning and I took their bow line. I had an early morning drink aboard her with Bob and Betsy. Bob sailed her over alone. I walked from here around to the beach along the coast this afternoon. The beach is ten minutes away by road but I spent an hour scrambling over lava boulders and investigating rock pools full of interesting things. Brightly coloured fish darted about over beautiful coral formations, shellfish spiny sea urchins and the biggest damn sea slug I've ever seen. I would not, and indeed without tools could not, break off a piece of living coral but I found a nice piece washed up on the beach.

Thursday August 9th

I had a guy from one of the charter boats come over this morning and ask if I wanted to make a few bucks. I agreed before even asking how much on doing what. I spent four hours piling rocks and gravel up to build a breakwater so that a slip they use wouldn't silt up so fast. It was hard work but I enjoyed the exercise, was well fed and made $20 cash. At 17:00 I got my anchor up and headed out of Manele Bay bound for the big city, Honolulu. I had to motor for the first few hours to clear the lee of Lanai. When I got wind it was just abaft the beam so she wouldn't self steer and I stayed at the helm all night.

Friday August 10th

At dawn the wind died down and I took in the jib and went below to sleep for half an hour. That brief nap and a strong cup of coffee set me back on my feet and I now had the island of Oahu in sight. The wind was astern so I set the twins and the wind promptly shifted to abeam. I struck the twins and set the other steering system only to have the wind then die. I fired up the seagull and ran it for about an hour then, when it ran out of gas, I decided to pull it aboard and check the gear oil. At the very moment that I pulled the retaining pin, a swell struck the stern awkwardly and the motor bounced off its mount and vanished overboard!! Naturally I had a line attached to it and quickly pulled it back aboard but it had been right underwater. I topped up the gear oil and gas and re-mounted it (carefully) but it would not start. I decided against pulling it apart out there rolling on the swells and sat waiting for wind. The wind, when it came, was a brisk 10-15 knots, again just abaft the beam and I sat at the helm as Diamond Head drew oh so slowly closer. We made the headland at about 14:00 then sailed past the famous Waikiki beach with its towering hotels. Just out from the Ala Wai boat harbour, I dropped sails and prepared to enter. Fenders out on both sides, dock lines fore and aft, two anchors, including the small one for throwing, set up in the cockpit, heaving line. I prepared for all eventualities as I knew not what to expect. Then I tried the motor. It started and ran smoothly. Inside the breakwater I tied her bow to a buoy and with the dinghy, took a line ashore to the breakwater. When I got ashore it was 17:00 and the harbour master's office was closed. I called customs then found a store and bought some ice cold beer. I ran into Terrell, a friend from Hilo and this evening he and I went to a bar for a couple of drinks.

Saturday August 11th

I checked in with the harbour master who I had been warned was a prize arsehole. He was but I finally got a berth. I spent the day chatting with people on boats, bought pilot charts of the south pacific and generally had a lazy day. Terrell and I bought a six pack of beer and sat around on his boat all evening. He has his boat up for sale right now with one very interested buyer, Frank Adams.

Sunday August 12th

I took the mainsail off this morning for the first time in over a year. I was impressed as no stitches had worn through and the only real damage was the batten pocket ends were worn and the nylon shackles holding the slides on need replacing. I met a guy from New Zealand who had some charts of New Zealand that he wanted to sell. I bought six of them plus a New Zealand pilot book for $20. Terrell took Frank out for a sail today and Frank is going to buy the boat. Frank took Terrell, a lady and I out for dinner tonight at the Hawaii Yacht Club. He paid.

Monday August 13th

I went back to the Hawaii Yacht Club today when the office opened and they will give me a berth. I moved Balandra around there under power and squeezed in between two bigger boats with a stern anchor down and the bow up to the sea wall. Lots of good people here, mostly cruisers and Balandra and I, as usual, get a lot of attention. Markeeta, the lady we had dinner with last night, came down to visit me this afternoon and stayed for a few hours but on a purely friendly basis (too bad).

Tuesday August 14th

I fitted new slide shackles to the mainsail, patched the batten pockets and refitted the main, now as good as new. I went up the mast as far as the forestay attachment and rove a dacron line through the ringbolt and secured it at the centre of its length. Each end of the line can now be run aft and secured when running with the twins, for extra support. This evening six of us gathered aboard 'Panacea', a Columbia 26, and played hearts until the early morning. There were Bob, Mark and Jay who sailed 'Panacea' over from the mainland, Christine from 'Bingo', Larry and I. I've not seen Terrell for a couple of days now.

Sunday August 19th

Life has been good here at the Hawaii Yacht Club, leaving little time for writing logs or letters. Tomorrow I leave and it will be with great sadness. The gang is breaking up; Mark and Jay flew to Kani and I may see them there, Mariline and Russ leave for Tahiti on Tuesday. 'Bingo' has the crew organised and is pulling out today. Terrell? He's still having problems finalising the deal with Frank, Bob is working here and 'Panacea' is up for sale and Larry on 'Darwin' will winter here. Life for the last week has been good. It's hard to go to sea again and be alone but it must be done. We are ready, the stores are all aboard, charts are bought and Balandra is fit and well. It would be so easy to linger. When can I settle and keep the friends I make.

Monday August 20th

We're at sea. The sun has just set and the lights of Honolulu are beginning to twinkle on the horizon. We're close reaching south east under double-reefed main. The wind is fairly light but a steep swell is running, making the motion uneasy. She's reefed right down as I don't feel in tune yet.

08:00 Tuesday August 21st

I slept well all night in half hour snatches. The motion improved as we came into the lee of Molokai, Lanai and Maui. The wind is now very light and I shook out the reefs this morning. There is no land in sight as we close reach east, south east over smooth seas. Things will get lumpy when we are to leeward of Alenuihaha channel but we may be far enough south by then to avoid the worst of it. I'm trying for lots of easting while still in the lee of the islands.

14:00 The wind is brisk out of the east, south east. We've two reefs back in the main and are pounding into the south. We are out of the island's lee and the seas are lumpy. Sometime tonight we should come into the lee of the big island. Hopefully, when we clear that, the wind will be more northerly. I snapped a horn off of a galvanised cleat holding the reefing line for the second reef. I was hauling hard on the line when the cleat broke and I almost went overboard!

18:00 We sailed into the lee of Hawaii a while ago and although the land is out of sight, the sea has settled and the wind all but died. What little breeze there is has shifted even more southerly and we're just able to make good a course of south, south west. We have bare steerageway but I've left a reef in the main as dark clouds are moving this way which may bring wind. I cut off most of my hair this afternoon. I only had a rusty pair of nail scissors and did it all by feel. When I was done and looked in the mirror it wasn't nearly as bad a job as I had thought it would be.

19:00 The wind has dropped and shifted more southerly and we're now headed west, south west. It matters little as we're just a breath away from being becalmed.

07:30 Wednesday August 22nd

We were becalmed last night with the ocean so still it was hard to tell the stars reflections from the phosphorescence. At 02:00, a long even swell began to roll in from the east and, an hour before dawn, the wind returned. I heard dolphins playing around us in the dark as I got sails up. Now the wind is brisk and gusty from the east, north east and we're close reaching south east with two reefs in the main. I have a pain in the gut today and have had the runs since dawn.

10:00 In a matter of minutes, the wind shifted around to east, south east and our heading is now south west. Motion has settled down as the swells are now from astern.

It's now after midnight and as I sip my hot tea with a nip of brandy, I can hear the dolphins calling me to come out and play. Squeaky little voices like a block needing oil called me from my bed an hour ago and I stayed outside whistling to them. Flashes of glittering phosphorescence, they came leaping and diving, squeaking and cavorting. My joy at being out there with them was dampened somewhat when a wave broke aboard and doused me from head to foot. Now I'm content to listen to them from within. We've been hard on the wind all day, barely making due south. We're heeled hard over and pounding through the swells, we're now making a few degrees of easting but it's heavy going and oh so wet. If the wind doesn't go more northerly by later today, I'll ease the sheets and head for Samoa. I'll not sail all the way to Fanning Island like this.

08:00 Thursday August 23rd

I slept very little last night. By dawn the wind had increased and I could no longer bear the pounding she was taking. I put a second reef in the main and put her on a beam reach heading south, south west. If the wind goes northerly in the next day or so we might still make Fanning. If not, I'll go for Samoa though that is a month's sailing. The wind is now east, south east but we should be getting north east trades for the next 500 miles.

20:00 We're now close reaching and making a few degrees east of south with the main still double-reefed. The motion is much easier and is worth a small loss of speed. In the twenty four hours until 14:00, we covered 110 miles. I'm impressed. I spent all day below, reading. The cockpit is a wet and comfortless place going to weather.

13:00 Friday August 24th

Another 100 miles to the south in the past twenty four hours. For a 20 foot boat going to weather under double-reefed main, that is great. We've gained a few miles of easting over yesterday's position. The wind is now east, north east.

10:00 Saturday August 25th

The wind increased during the night and as the apparent wind moved aft, we made more and more easting. By dawn, with everything reefed down, we were hard pressed but moving fast south east. Then suddenly the wind died. We rolled on the swells with very little wind for an hour or two but I left the reefs in. Dark rain clouds were approaching rapidly from the east, north east and I knew they would bring strong winds. As the clouds blotted out the sun, the wind laid us over and we're now pounding into the south, south east in heavy rain.

17:00 Another 90 miles made good and we're still inching eastward. We've had everything today from flat calms to double-reefed squalls, blazing sunshine to pouring rain. The real doldrums shouldn't start until we cross 10° north at the earliest and that's at least two days away. We're now making east, south east in light winds under full sail.

06:00 Sunday August 26th

Good progress until dawn but now the wind has died. Just after sunset last night, as I sat on deck with my after dinner coffee and brandy, a whale came to visit. I think he was a pilot whale. Shorter dorsal fin than a killer whale, black all over and only 10 to 12 feet long. He surfaced several times within 6 feet of us, keeping pace alongside.

14:00 Only 75 miles covered but solidly into the south east. The wind is now very, very light and every few minutes the sails collapse then fill again reluctantly with a snap. The sea is smooth with a trace of east, north east swell under sunny skies and puffy, white fair weather clouds. A picture postcard sky. 85° F in the cabin, comfortable enough. I spend most of my time below. It's a comfortable place and I stay out of the sun. I have to conserve body moisture. I bought lots of alcohol on this trip to see if it would allay boredom. It passes the time but I'm still bored. With my SW radio out of commission, I'm denied even the dubious pleasure of picking up any news. Hell, I've only been at sea a week. Today I am halfway to Fanning Island but I have yet to cross the doldrums. Balandra is behaving beautifully. I've hardly put a hand to her these last few days.

08:00 Monday August 27th

The wind is still very light and we're moving slowly south, south east.

12:00 70 more miles covered which is pretty good with the light winds we've had. Now the sails are slatting and I should probably take them down. Still we have a little way on into the south and that's better than nothing. There are fish swimming beneath Balandra. I first noticed them yesterday and set out a second fishing line but to no avail.

16:00 Becalmed since noon. I had a fish take a lure! A buzz bomb with a triple hook and an Oxo cube on the hook. I couldn't even begin to turn its head and it snapped the light (15 lb) line with ease. When free, it leapt clear of the water. It was a large yellow fin tuna. I killed my first real shark this afternoon. He was about my size, yellowy brown skin and a very squared-off head. I spotted him 30 feet off and swimming lazily toward us with his pilot fish in formation around his head. He was swimming on the surface and came right up to the boat at which time I sunk my harpoon between those sinister looking eyes. Mortally wounded and stunned, he swam a few feet but hauling gently on the harpoon line, I bought him alongside. Thinking the harpoon to be well set, I tried to lift his head with it to set to the gaff. The harpoon pulled out and he was gone, sinking away from me with a wriggling motion like a headless eel. I felt badly at having killed him and then being unable to even bring him aboard.

10:00 Tuesday August 28th

The wind returned at nightfall and held brisk and steady until early morning. There were a series of calms, squalls and rain culminating in my going on deck in the rain at 04:00 to put a reef in the main. Half an hour later, I had to get up again and sheet everything in tight as we were rolling in a flat calm. Since dawn the wind has been steady east, north east.

20:00 At sundown, I was doing the usual things, filling and lighting the backstay light, bringing the fishing lines aboard. Just as I reached for the second fishing line, something took the lure. It was a shark about 4 feet long and it put up very little fight until I tried to bring it aboard. Twice I tried and each time it would thrash and take off for a few yards then came tamely back alongside with very little coaxing on the line. The third time, I gaffed him squarely in the gills and hauling on the gaff and line, I had him halfway into the boat when, with a final desperate struggle, he broke the handle of the gaff and the 120 lb stainless leader where it was spliced to the hook. He was over the side and gone. Oh well, another lesson in shark catching.

10:30 Wednesday August 29th

An hour after sunset last night, the wind died and I dropped the sails. The dolphins came to play around us in the moonlight, leaping high and one even did a fancy somersault. I wonder why they only come at night? The wind came back at 02:00 and has held since then.

16:00 The wind is still holding. We've covered 160 miles in the past 48 hours. Very good, all things considered. We're now 330 miles from Fanning Island. I was toying with the idea of pushing on to Christmas Island but there is no real advantage and Fanning looks to be an easier landfall.

08:00 Thursday August 30th

Doldrums!! Last night there was a sudden squall with lots of rain, then the wind died and has not blown since. The sea is mirror smooth under a clear sky and it's already hot.

17:00 This is the hardest kind of sailing; for the boat and for me. I've had the sails up and down at least a dozen times today. Often just minutes after raising sail, the breeze dies and I let the sails slat for a while to see if the wind is coming back. Then, as soon as I drop them and go below, it will blow again. I took a fresh water shower in a rain squall today.

09:00 Friday August 31st

A breeze picked up yesterday evening and held steady all night from the east, north east. Now it is failing and is insufficient to keep the sails filled.

14:00 290 miles to go. The wind is very light and we just have steerageway with Gemini steering. We're now far enough south and have maintained enough easting that we should be able to run the rest of the way like this. Today is the first time that I have set the twins on this leg of the journey. When the breeze dies, it gets so very hot, it's 90° F in the cabin right now. I have my last two cans of beer in front of me now and that's the last I'll have for a while. I'm sure there are no supplies at Fanning except maybe fruit and coconuts. I'm also on my last paperback. I was given a stack of them by various people before leaving Hawaii. Even warm beer tastes awfully good.

09:00 Saturday September 1st

We're becalmed in the rain. By nightfall yesterday, the wind had shifted so far south that I had to take down the twins and use the main again. By midnight we were becalmed once more. The sky has been more heavily overcast since yesterday and last night, when the bright half moon poked through a gap in the clouds, I saw a moonbow for the first time ever.

16:00 No wind. We're sitting on a heaving, glassy sea. We've covered no more than 20 miles since yesterday. The rain stopped around noon and now it is hot. Damp, sticky, sweaty hot.

08:00 Sunday September 2nd

We have wind. Lots of it out of the south, along with solid overcast sky, poor visibility and pouring rain. We were becalmed all night and it rained and rained and rained. Dawn brought the wind and now we're pointing as high as we can go, with a reef in the main. The cloud cover is so dense that I barely have enough light to write by.

12:00 What a miserable day. We're still beating hard to windward in the pouring rain. The wind shifted to south west and I put her over on starboard tack for the first time in 2 weeks. The ever present deck leaks are letting in large quantities of water, despite my efforts in Honolulu. Two good points though; I've collected 5 gallons of rain water and my body is the cleanest it's been in two weeks.

18:00 Miserable, miserable day. The rain stopped a couple of times this afternoon but it has remained heavily overcast. The wind has been shifting constantly and varying a good deal in strength, keeping me busy adjusting sails and helm. I've changed tack at least eight times, which is no simple matter with the steering sail rigged. We're now heading south. I just went out and put a second reef in the main. The wind is making up for the days it missed. We're pounding hard into it with spray flying and leaks leaking. Miserable day. I guess I've been spoilt by all of the trade wind sailing.

09:00 Monday September 3rd

The wind died last night at about 22:00 so I dropped the sails and went to bed. I woke at midnight to find the wind blowing and a large sea bird sitting on the end of the boom. When I went on deck, I expected him to fly away but he just calmly looked at me and stayed put. I shouted at him and touched his tail but still he stayed. I was wary of putting my hands too close to that sharp-looking beak so I use a wooden spoon to poke him from his perch. He simply flew in a circle and landed back in the same spot. He was larger than a large seagull with white head and body, dark wings and long beak. I found that I could touch him without getting bitten. Now, this was all very nice but I couldn't hoist the sails with him there and my bed was getting cold so I pushed him from his perch and hoisted the main before he could return. Even then he flew in circles looking for another perch for some time. The wind was from the south, south west and the best course I could set was little south of west. That wind blew briskly and has held steady through until now. The sky cleared overnight and today the sun is shining once more.

14:00 The noon position is discouraging. We've made good only 120 miles in the past 5 days. We're now in the equatorial counter current which flows east so, every time the wind stops, we lose ground. Fanning Island is still 250 miles away and the wind right now is failing once more.

16:00 Totally becalmed once more.

09:00 Tuesday September 4th

The wind didn't return until 04:00 this morning and I got up then to raise sail. When raising the main, I haul rapidly on the halyard to start so that the head of the sail doesn't have a chance to blow forward and catch inside the lower shrouds.

The snap shackle fastening the halyard to sail somehow unfastened itself as I started to pull and the halyard end was at the masthead before I realised what had happened. I did the only thing possible in the circumstances and went back to bed to wait for daylight. At dawn I taped a fishing hook to the topping lift and started fishing. The block for the topping lift is just above the main halyard sheave and I thought I might be able to hook the errant shackle. I spent two hours trying from every position on the boat with two different sized hooks. Finally I got it. Before hoisting the main, I taped the guilty shackle so it couldn't open accidentally again. The wind this morning is a little more southerly and we're only about 10° west of our needed course. I wish it would go to the south east where it belongs.

13:00 We've lost 15 miles since noon yesterday. We're 15 miles east and a little south of our last position. That's partly the current but also we must have been blown a few miles off of our course this morning before I was able to get the sails up. I also lost my favourite sponge overboard this morning whilst rinsing it over the side. I tried to recover it but the wind was very light and manoeuvring was difficult and I soon lost sight of it. I have a couple of spares but that was the best one.

10:00 Wednesday September 5th

The wind died last night at 21:00 so I dropped the sails and went to bed. Within an hour the wind came up out of the north west and we got under way on a starboard tack. An hour later, that wind died and I dropped the sails again. At 02:00, the south, south west wind came back and, by 04:00, I had to put a reef in the main. By dawn I had a second reef in the main and now we're pounding through a lumpy sea, hard on the wind. I still can't point far enough south to set a course for Fanning. We're steering a little west of south west now.

16:00 All morning the wind increased and the seas built up and we ploughed through them. The south west seas superimposed on the ever present easterly swells which made for a very uncomfortable ride. By 14:00 she could not hold her course and the motion below was intolerable. I dropped the jib and since then we have been jogging along into the west with much easier motion and less strain on the rigging. With the current flowing against me and the wind right in my teeth, progress is very slow. Since noon yesterday we have made good only 40 miles and we have had to work for every one of them.

18:00 The wind has dropped a little and shifted more westerly. Before sundown I'll put her over on starboard tack and try for some southing. I just checked the pilot chart and I'm comforted to discover that the wind never blows from the south west in this part of the ocean. It has an easterly component more that 80% of the time – apparently!

10:00 Thursday September 6th

We sailed hard on the wind all night on starboard tack with the main double-reefed. During the night, the wind died right away and I dropped the jib and steering sail. I had just gone back below when a squall hit with torrential rain and strong winds. It only lasted a few minutes and left us with a light south westerly wind so I went on deck to hoist the other sails. I just had the steering sail up when the rain started and the wind increased. By the time I had got back to the cockpit it was blowing at least 40 knots and the rain was hissing down, flattening the seas with its force. Visibility was down to a few yards and Balandra was flying. The driving rain stung my naked skin so painfully that I had to go below. Within a few minutes, it passed. I hoisted the jib and we continued pounding to windward with strong winds.

By morning, the wind had gone more southerly and I put her about onto port tack. The wind is still 20 knots or more and we're slamming and pounding into the south west – a comfortless way to sail. Everything below is damp and with all of the spray flying, I have to keep the main hatch closed, making it hot and stuffy in the cabin. I have a sore or boil forming at the base of my spine from so many days spent in my 'going to windward' position. That is, back against the cabinet, tail bone on the rug and feet up high, braced against the far side of the boat. The constant salty damp doesn't help. If the wind doesn't shift in the next day or two, we're going to miss Fanning Island. It just has to shift easterly soon.

13:00 I give up, I quit, let me off, I want to go home. After a mere 24 hours of slogging to windward, being awake most of the night, getting everything wet and having my body soaked and shaken, where does it get me? We have lost 17 miles since yesterday noon. The equatorial counter current must be something fierce. In the last nine days we've made good only 170 miles. If there was any place else to head for I would but even Samoa is to the south of the course we're on now. So we carry on, thump, thump, splash, thump, splash into the south west. Please change wind, please.

09:00 Friday September 7th

Another cheerless night has passed lying sleepless on my damp bed. Always a new dawn is the hope of man and as I stood watching the sunrise, a large school of dolphins came by to brighten my day. They stayed with us for maybe an hour and then, as suddenly, they were gone. When the sun was high enough, I took a sight and joy of joys, WE HAVE MADE PROGRESS!!!! I won't know exactly how much until I get a noon sight to cross it with but I'd say about 70 miles. The wind is still strong, out of the south and with the main still double-reefed, we're making west, south west. What we need to steer is south, south west.

13:00 80 miles made good since yesterday noon. 150 miles to go but we'll miss Fanning if the wind doesn't shift. Either that or we make a long tack back to the south east. We'll see. The wind dropped a little and I shook out both reefs. To celebrate such good mileage, I'm going to dig through the bilge and find something special to eat. I'm also going to try and dry my pillow and sheet now that we have less spray flying.

17:00 I couldn't find anything very inspiring to eat so I settled for a can of beef ravioli and a can of potatoes followed by a can of peaches. I also made up one of my instant chocolate pudding mixes using skimmed milk powder. They usually set funny and taste a little odd but as us old salts say, "better a funny chocolate pudding than no chocolate pudding". The wind finally shifted. Not much but enough that we can now steer comfortably for Fanning. If the wind will only hold for a couple of days, we'll be there by this time on Sunday. This little 1,000 mile jaunt has turned into quite an epic voyage. I expected it to take 2 weeks at the most and today is my nineteenth day at sea. Since losing sight of Honolulu I have not seen one sign of the existence of mankind. Not a ship, plane or even so much as a piece of garbage. My radio has not worked since before Hawaii (it got wet) and I've had no news this whole trip. Civilization could have been destroyed, creatures from outer space could have landed, the US president could have been caught with his fingers in the till and I wouldn't know. Bit spooky.

09:00 Saturday September 8th

The wind is now solidly out of the south east at about 10 knots and we're moving well, right on course. The wind fell very light during the night and the sea flattened out. I slept well. That, of course, still means waking up many times to check course and wind and to look at the moon and stars. I saw a most beautiful moonrise last night, huge and golden, rising beneath a bank of cloud. Last night it was a day past full moon. I was also up at dawn to watch the sunrise.

13:00 Another 75 miles covered and 75 to go. The wind is fairly light right now but we should make Fanning tomorrow with no problem.

19:30 The wind has been very light all afternoon but now, as darkness closes in it is freshening. The moon won't rise until about 22:00 tonight. The way things look now, I should have Fanning Island in sight by mid-morning (if I can find it). It's a small, low island and I'll have to get within 10-12 miles before I'll be able to see it.

07:00 Sunday September 9th

When will I learn not to predict landfall. We are becalmed. During the night the wind fell lighter and lighter until, by 04:00, it was so light that it wasn't blowing at all. I have the sails back up now to catch each vagrant puff that comes our way but they are mostly just slatting and wearing themselves out. If there is no wind by the time I've taken and marked a sun sight, I'm going to pull out the motor.

17:00 Damned if I can see the bloody thing. I've motored for many hours today and have seen many things but no land. The noon position put me about 25-30 miles north of it and I would not have reached it before dark anyway but I ought to be able to see it by now. The whole horizon to the south is rained in and visibility that way is probably 3 or 4 miles. Right now I have a little wind and therefore a break from sitting at the helm. Even as I write this, the wind is dying again. I'll have to lie ahull for the night but I'd like to see the island first for peace of mind. The sails are slatting back to the helm and the motor.

False alarm, the wind is now very light but we're still moving. It's about an hour and a half until sundown and I'm hoping the horizon may clear a little before then. All day we motored over glassy seas, first in hot sunshine, then pouring rain, now solid overcast. A school of pilot whales came to play and have their pictures taken. I noticed a number of odd-looking creatures on the surface, like tiny deformed jellyfish. Scooping one up in a pail, I poked him with my finger which came away with tiny blue threads adhered to it. I rubbed it with my thumb to clean it off and experienced immediate pain, like a bee sting in both finger and thumb. The pain lasted about an hour but even now it throbs a little. That'll teach me to mess with defenceless creatures.

A little later I spotted what looked like an avocado with fins. I circled around and scooped it up in the pail (I didn't touch it though). It was the oddest, ugliest looking fish. I don't know if it was sick or dying but it just floated there on its side with little fins flapping slowly and didn't respond when I poked it (with dish mop handle this time). I took its picture and returned it to the ocean. What else did I see. Oh yes! A leaf from a tree. Just a very small and brown leaf but a definite sign of land. I just managed to get a sun sight through a break in the cloud. As far as I can figure, unless my navigation is way off, I should be within ten miles of Fanning and to the north of it. To the south of me though is where the lowest, thickest, blackest, wettest clouds are. Also the wind is now out of the south. I've taken the sails down and I'm going to sit here for a while and see what happens.

06:00 Monday September 10th

Dawn at last. All night it has rained and rained but now .... it's still raining. The slowly gathering light shows a grey and formless world with indistinct horizons. I could sail by 2 miles from land and not see it. At times like this I find myself asking "What am I doing here?". If I can't find the island today then I'm going to head right for Samoa. Dammit, I'll find it.

08:30 I've been at the helm for the past one and a half hours in the pouring rain. My poor naked body is so wrinkled now. Now I have a steering line rigged to the cabin so I can steer and be dry whilst using the interior compass. Visibility is about 3 miles all around and no sign of the cloud cover breaking up. I'm going to motor south until 11:00 then stop. If the sun doesn't come out for a noon sight then it will be hopeless to just keep motoring around.

11:30 A person could begin to get discouraged. The sky is still solid overcast with the southern horizon blackest of all. At least the rain has stopped for a while. I got one sight. Just a lighter patch behind the clouds brought down to a hazy horizon but any sight is better than none. The LINE OF POSITION obtained runs north to south, almost through the island, so I guess it's due south of me. The problem now is that a stiff wind has come up right out of the south so we're beating, beating, beating to windward once more. I have no way of knowing how far north I am unless I can get a noon latitude. Failing that, I'll keep tacking one and a half hours each way and maybe I'll run into it!

14:00 At noon, the clouds gathered more densely to make sure that I wouldn't get a sight. The cloud cover is still complete and now the wind has fallen very light and it's raining once more. The wind has kicked up enough of a sea that it's too lumpy to motor in. What now? I really don't want to go straight on to Samoa. That would be another 2-3 weeks at sea and I have no fresh fruit, vegetables or snacks. Water is also low although I can manage with what I have even without catching any rain. It's mainly that this will be my only chance to see a real pacific, coral island, an attol in fact. The wind has died now and I'd better take down the sails.

16:00 I motored in the rain for a couple of hours but all there is to see is rain and clouds and empty ocean. There is no wind now and the rain is still coming down. I now have no real idea where I am, it's all guesswork. I could be going away from land for all I really know. I'm going to sit here until morning and see if it brings sunshine. The danger there is that the current could carry me far away by tomorrow. Well, I can do no more. I can't sail without wind so here I sit.

18:30 After a bite to eat, I got lucky and through a break in the cloud I took a good sight. It still ran basically north to south passing close to Fanning Island and since I was sure I couldn't be south of it yet, it followed that the island must still be to the south of me. The cloud cover had thinned and raised up and the sea was fairly calm with no wind so I fired up the motor and ran for another hour due south. This did no good at all and now, as the evening draws on, we are sitting once more an a glassy sea. Now I hope that the wind doesn't blow tonight. We'll just sit here quietly and wait for sunrise and please, oh please, let the sky be clear tomorrow.

20:00 I just picked up the little transistor radio to see if I could pick anything up. I've got an AM station loud and clear. The song that was playing when I tuned in was 'Island Love' – appropriate!! I can't believe that Fanning Island, with a population of 400, would have AM radio. The news just came on and it's a Hawaiian station. Must just be a fluky reception. That's the first thing I've picked up since about 3 days out from Hawaii.

08:00 Tuesday September 11th

Well, another day and the sky is clearing, the sun is shining and I've been up since before dawn trying to fix our position. There is not a breath of wind and there hasn't been all night. The ocean is flatter than I've ever seen it. All of the LOPs I'm getting run north to south and I'll have to wait until noon to get a proper latitude. Everything I have got so far indicates that

Fanning Island is due south and only about 10-12 miles away. So, once more I'll motor south for 2-3 hours and if I don't find it, I'll wait for noon. I've used more fuel in the last two days than on the whole trip so far.

10:30 The wind came up an hour ago and blew hard right out of the south. It didn't blow for long, just long enough to move masses of heavy, grey clouds overhead and then leave them there. It is now raining and the wind has all but died away.

13:00 The sky cleared before noon and I got my long-awaited noon latitude. We are surprisingly still 24 miles north of Fanning and a little to the west. There is just a very faint breeze out of the south right now and we're motoring along under sunny skies. We'll be lucky to reach there by sundown but I won't mind another night out here if I have the island in sight.

18:00 Oh hell. We've been going non-stop for five hours, motoring then sailing, when an east wind came up. I took down the steering sail and sat at the helm to get maximum speed. Now, even if we had averaged as little as 3 knots, land should be in sight by now. It ain't. I think I am fated not to make this landfall. I'm going to eat now and then sit at the helm well into the night, if the wind holds. I only have enough fuel left for about 3 hours motoring.

20:00 It's a black and moonless night and I'm getting scared. Balandra is steering herself and romping along hard on the wind. I could be up on the beach before I even saw the damned island. It would be my kind of sailing to find it like that. I just re-read the pilot book and it says that Fanning is visible from 15 miles out from the deck of a ship. Now they're not talking about Balandra. I just looked up my 'Distance of Visibility of Objects at Sea' tables (honestly) and something 80 feet high should be visible from sea level from 10.3 miles. I think I'll sail for one more hour then stop and wait until the moon comes up.

23:00 We're inching along under reefed mainsail into the south. The night sky is clear and filled with stars but they are more for show than illumination. The moon should rise in about an hour and be a little better than half full. I'm tired but I dare not sleep. Tonight seemed an appropriate time to study the taking and use of star sights. They have to be taken close to dusk or dawn, when the horizon is visible. At dawn I'll try my hand, though I'm not sure that my sextant is powerful enough for stars or planets. I've tried moon shots but they are very complex and tedious and never come out right.

05:30 So much for star sights at dawn. It's pouring with rain out of an overcast sky right now. All night we've moved slowly to and fro across the wind ever eastward and southward.

06:30 The dawn has brought...... nothing. No stars, no sun, no wind, no land, just a disgusting swell that rolls us outrageously. Most of the horizon is veiled by rain and clouds. I'm no further ahead than I was three days ago, in fact, I'm down about 5 gallons of fuel, 3 day's food and a bunch of sleep. Today is absolutely the last day.

08:00 Wednesday September 12th

The south east wind is blowing and we're beating into it heading south. I've no idea where we are, so south is as good as any direction. If we find it, great, if not at least we're headed in the right general direction for Samoa.

14:00 The sun came out in time for a noon latitude and I think I know where I am. I look to be about 17 miles east of land, passing it by. We're hard over on the starboard tack now and we'll have one last shot at it. The sky is clear now and it's hot,

hot, hot. I'm very, very tired and I'm going to try and sleep for an hour now.

16:30 After my nap, I checked the horizon and there was nothing. So I took and marked another sun sight then checked the horizon, nothing. I had a shower and washed my hair, then checked the horizon, zilch. Now I've promised myself I won't peek again for half an hour. If it's not in sight before dark then there is something definitely wrong with my navigation. If I don't find it by sundown then I guess I turn around and leave, defeated. That will make me very unhappy but I don't see much sense in drifting around here any longer. I've been at sea for 24 days now and here to Samoa is as far as from Hawaii to here. Mind you, from here on I expect better winds. Even so, it will be at least a two week passage. Oh please let me find Fanning Island. Please, please.

17:30 This is so frustrating I could cry. I've already been through the screaming and cursing stage and now I could just cry. All of my sights indicate that the island should be dead ahead and within 5 miles by now, at most. In fact, some of my calculations had me hard aground half an hour ago. The sky is clear, the horizon nice and sharp and empty.

21:00 I couldn't do it. I couldn't quit and let a little chunk of coral in the middle of the ocean defeat me. Right now we're sailing a little east of north and in the morning we'll run back down to the south and try once more to spot the elusive island. I'll have to stay awake once more so that we don't find the land unexpectedly. Sometime after midnight, when the moon is up, I'll let her drift and nap for a while.

09:00 Thursday September 13th

I blew it. I fell asleep and she ran on for many miles more than I had intended. Now it'll probably take me most of the day to

sail back. The sun's declination being basically the same as my latitude, I can still only get north to south LOPs and will have to wait until noon to get a proper fix.

13:00 I'm either having colossal bad luck or I'm a really stupid navigator. I think some of each. I fixed my position at noon, got a lot of good sights and I'm sure the fix is right. Unfortunately!!! I'm now 80 miles north of Fanning. 80 miles! Now I'm sure I didn't cover that distance last night, so my noon sight yesterday must have been wrong. So, for 2 days I've sailed the wrong way. As soon as I discovered where I was, the brisk easterly wind shifted south and fell very light to further impede my progress. I swear I'm fated not to visit Fanning Island.

19:00 Becalmed. The wind died at 16:00 and I motored for one and a half hours but now we're rolling hard on glassy seas. I'm down to my last gallon of fuel so that's it for the motor, except in and out of port until Samoa. I took stock today and the food is holding up OK but it's all basic, canned goods. There are no fancy foods, snacks or sweet treats left. The only meats left are one can each of tuna and corned beef. Some fresh fruit would be most welcome as would a fish or two. Water would be my only real concern if I didn't stop at Fanning. I stupidly passed many opportunities to fill all of the containers through over-confidence in my ability to find a tiny island. I have only 9 gallons left. Today I checked myself to see how much fresh water I drank and was amazed. I rationed myself fairly strictly yet still drank a good three quarters of a gallon.

09:30 Friday September 14th

Not a breath of wind all night. At 07:30, a breeze from the south west came up and blew for 15 minutes. A while later, a breeze came up from the south east. Back up with the sails, this time for about 30 minutes. Since then I've changed tacks four times and now have the sails down again. I was able to collect about a gallon of water during a brief rain squall and I feel good about that, although 10 gallons would have suited me better.

18:00 Well I didn't collect 10 gallons but I've collected more than 5 gallons of rainwater in the last 2 hours. There was a little bit of wind with the rain and we made a few miles to the south. Other than that, I sat and wrote letters all day with no wind to preoccupy me. Right now, the wind has died again though it is still raining. It's impossible to collect rainwater with no wind as the rain has to be driven against the mainsail.

19:00 The wind picked up half an hour ago out of the south west and it's blowing steadily at 10-15 knots. We're moving well due south but I don't think it will last. A south westerly wind has no business blowing here it should be south east. Yesterday and today I've been using the genoa for the first time since San Francisco. I'd forgotten how much higher we could point with the genny set but it's a real handful changing tacks with that steering sail in the way and we also heel a lot more. This evening I feel better than I've felt in a while. I have a full belly, full water tank, full sails and a full quota of sleep last night. It surely will be nice to get the anchor down in a calm lagoon and get some real sleep though.

20:30 The wind has died and the sails are down.

06:30 Saturday September 15th

Before dawn I woke to find a light south west wind blowing. I hoisted all sail and we're now moving slowly south. On nights like last night and the night before, I get up every hour, with the aid of the alarm clock, to check conditions. With no sails up, a light wind could blow for hours unnoticed.

15:00 All day the south west wind has blown, sometimes harder, sometimes softer. The sky has been overcast all day and I was unable to get a noon sight. The LOPs I have got show that we drifted 40 miles or more easterly while becalmed last night!! It's hard to believe but true. So, all day we've been hard on the wind, pounding along but still unable to steer our desired course. I feel like I'm doomed to sail towards Fanning Island forever without getting there. This morning I collected another one and a half gallon of water and we're now in good shape once more. I had been worried in case we couldn't make Fanning but now I don't care. This afternoon I made cookies! I mixed together porridge oats, granola, wheat germ, brown sugar, margarine, chocolate powder and a little milk. When the mixture was good and gooey, I dropped a spoonful at a time into the frying pan with a little margarine and flattened into cookie shape. They came out looking like overdone hamburgers but they surely are the best cookies I've had in a month at least.

18:30 Another day draws to a close and we have a few miles behind us. How many and where we are now I know not. The wind shifted to the west and then a little north of west and we're now steering our desired course. A short time ago a squall of such ferocity struck that I felt obliged to take down the sails for a while. The sky remained overcast all day and it has not been pleasant but at least it's wind.

08:00 Sunday September 16th

The wind held all night from north of west but now it has died and we are becalmed once more. Twice during the night we were hit by squalls and I had to take down the genoa. The sky this morning is solidly overcast and I don't know where we are.

12:30 No noon sight, no wind, no position, no progress, nothing. Just the heavy, infuriatingly constant rolling and the creak of the rigging. A person could get desperate (though it would do them no good). The highlight of the day was having a 5 foot shark bang up against the rudder. He left before I could bring the harpoon to bear.

14:30 Things are looking up. The sky has cleared, the sun is shining and Gemini is maintaining bare steerageway before a light south easterly wind. Although we steered our course all night, the current has set us 40 miles easterly. Fanning Island is now due west, which makes a change anyway.

20:00 There are other people in the world. I saw a ship. At 17:00, a large container ship with PAD in large (huge) letters on its side passed about 3 miles ahead of us. The wind has remained light and shifted more southerly. I had to take down the twins and we're now beam reaching due west with Fanning

Island 40 miles away. I'd say we'll be there by morning if I didn't know better. We won't make it, no way. We'll never get there by tomorrow. Today I've been reading 'Advanced First Aid Afloat' for lack of anything else as yet unread. I now know how to treat a crewman for a ruptured appendix, set a broken bone, and recognise and treat heatstroke. All I need is two more people on board and a complete pharmacy.

04:00 Monday September 17th

The wind is brisk and steady out of the south. We were moving so fast that I put a reef in the main at midnight for fear of running past Fanning in the dark. Even so, I've been up since 02:00 keeping watch. There is lightning on the northern horizon beneath heavy black clouds. The sky overhead and to the south and west is clear and in the east, a tiny paring of a moon is struggling to climb above the cloud bank. I shall be glad to see the dawn.

05:00 I smell land. I can see nothing yet but dawn is near. If I can smell it then it is to windward. I've dropped the jib and I'll wait and see what daylight brings.

06:30 As the eastern sky brightened, I perceived a dark outline across the horizon to the south. I also became aware of a constant low rumble of surf on the shore. As the sun rose, the land was revealed less than 1 mile distant. We're now sailing parallel to the shore, half a mile off, in light wind just soaking up the greenery. The island is very low and densely wooded with coconut palms and other luxuriant growth. The sunshine on the greenery is a delight to the eye after 4 weeks of blues and greys and white. We have 3-4 miles to sail around the coast to get to English Harbour, the only entrance to the lagoon. The current can run through the pass there at up to 7 knots. I approach it with some trepidation but if we can't get through, we simply wait until the tide changes.

11:30 We're in, anchored and cleared already. The local policeman came out in a boat with a couple of other natives and cleared me. They have a store here and I'm going ashore to see what goodies I can find.

16:30 The store was closed. I met a Gilbert islander named Joseph who took me to his house to meet his wife and drink tea. I also met Bill Frew, an Australian who is the copra plantation manager. The plantation is the island and everybody works for the company. I had two cold beers in Bill's office and came back to Balandra to sleep them off. I'm invited to join Bill at his house at 17:30 for drinks so I'd better get moving.

09:00 Tuesday September 18th

I had supper at Bill's house along with copious quantities of cold Australian beer. Bill has a Gilbertese wife and three children though they did not eat with us. He has a houseboy who does the cooking, dishes etc. I enjoyed a very pleasant evening and I'm sure Bill enjoyed talking to somebody from 'outside'. They have a generator here for power but they only run it from sundown until 22:00. At 22:00 I made my way back to the dinghy with the aid of a borrowed flashlight. At the jetty, there is a night watchman to watch over the boats.

He greeted me and watched me row away and ten minutes later, watched me row back. The tidal current was so strong that I couldn't make any headway towards Balandra. The old watchman told me that the tide would turn in an hour so I sat in the dark with him and we shared a cup of tea from his thermos. I finally reached Balandra at 23:30. Twice during the night I woke with a start wondering at the lack of motion. Ah yes, I'm at anchor.

Wednesday September 19th

I had lunch at Bill's house yesterday but then, instead of going back to the office, Bill took the afternoon off and we sat on the veranda drinking beer. He told me how he has not left the island in 5 years but now is planning to go on leave. The problem, he said, is that the company in Sydney can find no one to relieve him. So he offered me the job!! Subject to approval from Sydney. It didn't take me long to accept. After all, if I have to work, why not do it on a tropical island in mid-pacific. Bill figures that I can earn around $10,000 Australian a year and would pay only about 10% income tax. The house (which is huge and old) is free. The only living expense is food and booze which is bought in by ship every 3 to 6 months. So, today, Bill will telegram Sydney and seek their approval. It is, after all, somewhat unorthodox to pick up somebody who is sailing through and make him plantation manager. In a few days we'll get a reply. This morning I'm going to borrow Bill's small sailing dinghy and explore the lagoon.

07:30 Thursday September 20th

It is solid overcast with pouring rain and a brisk north east wind blowing but I don't care. I'm snug and dry with a shot of rum in my morning coffee just like in the good old days. Bill's boat was a wreck. The boat itself was in good shape and Bill uses it occasionally with a small outboard motor on it. It hadn't been sailed for six years but we dug the spars and sails out of the cobwebs under the house and I began putting it together. There were pieces broken and parts missing but with some blocks and spare line from Balandra and odd bits of wire and string, I put her in sailable shape. She's a gaff-rigged cat boat, old fashioned and alien to me. 12 feet long, clinker built with flat bottom and centreboard. The sail is old and baggy but she'll go to windward, eventually. I didn't go far yesterday as it was late in the day when I had got her together. If I stay here, I get to use her and I can put my outboard on her to commute. Later today I'll explore the island on the other side of the pass for a more sheltered and secure anchorage.

18:00 What can I say. The island is beautiful. The lagoon is teeming with fish, the coconuts are delicious, there are land crabs aplenty that I'm told are good eating and the fridge is kept full of cold beer (just in the manager's house of course). I drifted around in Bill's boat for most of the day, exploring beaches and finding a good anchorage. Tomorrow I'll move Balandra over to the other side of the pass and anchor in a sheltered bay there. Bill is then going to lend me an outboard motor to get to and fro. The water runs through that pass at up

to 5 knots and trying to row or sail across it, a person could get swept right out of the lagoon. It's not really dangerous but most inconvenient. I'm borrowing Bill's motor because I don't want to unbolt my motor mount until we get an affirmative reply from Sydney. I hope they give me the job.

Friday September 21st

I moved Balandra across the pass at slack water. I caught a small fish for bait then hooked into a large one but it got away as usual. I spent the evening in Bill's company then stayed the night at his house as it was raining and we didn't want to mess with the outboard in the dark.

Saturday September 22nd

I fitted the outboard this morning and returned to Balandra. Last night was my first away from the boat since early April. Somebody had gone out to Balandra in a canoe and left two chicken eggs in the cockpit. Eggs are a precious commodity here and thus, it was a worthy gift. I suspect my friend Joseph. I returned to Bill's house in the evening to attend an island feast. Bill received a telegram from Sydney today. I got the job. Not only that but they're going to pay me $12,000 Australian a year. That's unbelievable. Experienced managers make no more that that apparently. I start work on Monday. In the evening, we went to the island gathering with flower garlands on our heads and ate chicken, rice and corned beef with our fingers while many speeches were made and songs were sung. Bill introduced me but said nothing about me working here as we have yet to organise a work permit. I spent the night at Bill's again due to heavy rain.

Sunday September 23rd

After breakfast this morning, Bill's family went off to church and Bill and I opened a couple of cold beers. We sat and drank all day as it was pouring with rain (as good an excuse as any). At 16:00 when the rain stopped, I headed back to Balandra.

19:30 I just had an islander come alongside in his canoe and ask permission to come aboard. He tied up and told me it was he who had left the eggs and now he had brought me a chicken. He was a young guy, 25 years old and built like a boxer. His English was passable as he had worked on ships from Australia to Canada. The chicken was still alive so he killed it by biting its head and cleaned it over the side, in the dark, by feel. He didn't overstay his welcome and was soon on his way.

Saturday September 29th

Today is the first day I've spent any time on Balandra since last weekend. I've worked all week but have yet to do anything. I'm getting paid but I can't 'officially' start work until I get a work permit. I'm therefore maintaining a low profile and spending my time in a corner of the office reading all of the files. Although telegrams were sent to Sydney and Tarawa on Monday regarding the work permit, no reply has been received as yet. I hope that there is no problem as I'd hate to have this deal fall through now. I've been taking all of my meals at Bill's house and sleeping there. This suits me and seems to please Bill as he's always encouraging me to stay and coming up with reasons for me not to go back to the boat. He has a cook and two house girls so it's no strain on his wife who also encourages me to feel at home. I now know a dozen or more people by name and two or three words in Gilbertese. The people are friendly, kind and gentle.

Sunday September 30th

I spent last night at Bill's and came back to Balandra this morning for a change of clothes. I have to be respectable for Sunday lunch. Marty from Honolulu is coming to lunch and

I look forward to meeting him. He flies down here every 6-8 weeks to do research for the University of Hawaii.

Monday October 22nd

I'm settling in to a new lifestyle that is soon to be disrupted. The manager on Washington Island, Merv Fagg, died a couple of weeks ago and I'm going to the island to take over for a while. There is a salvage tug on its way to the island via here to salvage some lead from a wreck on the coast there. It should be here at Fanning before the end of the week and I'll go to Washington on it. We're expecting our next ship here, the Vili, about mid-November. We hope to have a new man come in then to take over from me so I can return, relieving Bill, so that he and his family can go out on leave on the Vili. If a new man for Washington cannot be found in time, then I will have to remain on Washington until the next ship in January.

The Washington Island manager died under somewhat strange circumstances and the police wish to investigate as soon as they can get a police inspector there. Merv had been drinking heavily, very heavily for a couple of months and was in very bad shape. He wouldn't come on the radio for weeks at a time and when he did he would be drunk and unable to put even simple sentences together. Finally he came on the radio one day sober and we figured that maybe he had run out of booze. For two days he didn't drink, then he was found dead in his bathroom at 10:00 under the running shower. A piece of broken glass was embedded deeply into his calf muscle and he had bled to death.

The 'accident' apparently happened at around 02:00 outside the house. A window was broken and there was blood on the ground. He couldn't have put his foot through the window as it was too high and he had no reason to be breaking in as the door was never locked. The trail of blood led upstairs to the veranda where he apparently sat at the table for a while, then to the bedroom where he lay on the bed bloodying it, then to the bathroom. He made no attempt to summon help, remove the glass or stop the bleeding. He had not been drinking although there was still one bottle of liquor left in the house. A true mystery that neither we nor the police have been able to unravel over the radio, although I do have my own theory.

No office work has been done for at least two months and the books will be a real mess. The payroll hasn't been done for over a month and the men have been getting cash advances through the store keeper (with Bill's authorisation). It will be a mess but I'm looking forward to it in a masochistic sort of way.

I took Balandra's mast down and hauled her out. Unfortunately, the only place I could do this was on the other side of the pass and she cannot be seen from here. Vandalising someone's personal property is almost unheard of here but if I ran afoul of somebody as manager and they wanted to get back at me, Balandra would be a tempting target.

I have very little work to do here right now as Bill still does all of the office work. I walk around and show my face a couple of times a day to keep everyone on their toes, especially the carpenters who are pretty slack through lack of supervision. I try to show them easier and faster ways of doing things but response is slow as they are set in their ways. Everything is, of course, done with hand tools and that slows things down considerably.

Today I patched up the fibreglass sheathing on one of our wooden surf boats but, as a rule, I do almost no physical work. I designed a couple of houses last week and work was started on one of them today.

The evenings are passed pleasantly on Bill's veranda drinking cold Australian beer and yarning or just watching the surf break at the entrance to the pass. Bill's wife, Marina, is trying hard to marry me off to one of the house girls and this leads to much light-hearted (I hope) jesting. We eat very well, predominantly fish, though, on special occasions we'll have chicken or eggs. On real festive occasions a pig gets killed, as when the secretary to the minister for the Line Islands and the manager of the Christmas Island plantation, Perry Langston, came to visit for a couple of days a week ago. Locally grown produce includes breadfruit, bananas, papayas, mangoes (out of season now), limes, taro, pandanus and, of course, coconuts.

Wednesday October 25th

There is still no news of the salvage tug 'Salvador'. We've had no reply to our telegrams asking for news from Fiji and all we have is a rumour that the tug is at Canton Island. We've also had no news from Sydney as to whether they have a man for Washington Island coming in on the 'Vili'. In case I'm stuck on Washington until January, I ordered some stores today from Fiji to come in on the Vili. I kept the order to a bare minimum as Suva prices are notoriously high and if Bill goes out on the Vili I'll be taking over his stores ordered ex Sydney. I now have my first full month of work in here and have worked that out to be $862.50 after tax. Tax comes out to about $1,650 per annum which is pretty good out of $12,000. I'll be paid quarterly in Sydney and will arrange with Burns Philp to have most of my money deposited in a company staff account paying over 11% per annum. I have to leave enough money on the company books to cover any stores that I order and any cash advances I get here.

The salvage tug 'Pacific Salvador' finally arrived at Fanning last Sunday and left on Monday evening with Bill and I aboard for Washington Island. We arrived at Washington on Tuesday morning but couldn't land through the main passage as the surf was so bad. We finally, 11:00, landed on the north shore through moderate surf and rode a tractor into the settlement. The tug returned to Fanning the same evening with Bill aboard and I was left alone with my new people.

Saturday November 3rd

Today, except for two hours on the radio with Bill trying to work out the books, I did no work. I sat drinking beer and reading all day. All week I've been spending from 07:00 until well into the evening trying to make some sense out of the mess in the office. Merv Fagg, the late manager, had done nothing for months but sit around the house in an alcoholic stupor. According to people here, he would start drinking when he woke up and then drink until he passed out. He drank scotch and bourbon straight from the bottle and consumed up to three (yes, three!) bottles a day. Some of the people had not had a proper pay cheque since July although, with Bill's authorisation, the storeman, Beiata, had been giving cash advances where needed. I now have all of the August payroll completed and September and October pay will be paid out on Monday if I work all day tomorrow. Many people had errors in their pay going back as far as June. Allowances that were due and not paid and so forth. I hope to have all of the pay correct and up to date by the middle of next week. After that, I'll try to untangle and update the rest of the books and records. The people are very happy to have a new (and sober) manager and since my arrival, fish, eggs, papayas and a whole stem of bananas have appeared at the house. I bought a fellow with me from Fanning named Tabeaua (pronounced Tabby oh a) to be my cook and butler! He used to be a steward on a ship and speaks passable English. Also, I have two house girls Mamele (Ma milly) and Eretia (Erisia) to keep the house clean and do my laundry and ironing. When I moved in, I inherited a thin, battle-scarred but affectionate old cat who is now curled up asleep at my feet.

Last night a party was held in my honour in the protestant church maneaba (an open-sided hall). Traditional Gilbertese food was served and I was praised for eating with my hands in island style and not asking for a knife and fork. The food was served on banana leaf platters as we sat cross-legged on mats spread around the maneaba's concrete floor. Before we ate, Kabure gave a speech thanking me for attending along with many kind words. Kabure is chairman of 'The Old Man of the Peace' which makes him like a mayor. After the food, the protestant and catholic pastors both made speeches and then I made mine. I had Taukoban (the foreman) beside me to translate and I thanked the people for their patience and co-operation through such a trying and unsettled period. Kabure made another speech and then I was presented with a beautiful, hand-woven sleeping mat 6 foot by 3 foot in size. It is a fine weave with an intricate design. The protestant pastor's (John Ben) wife had started it when I arrived on Tuesday and apparently just got it finished in time for the party.

After the speeches had been patiently listened to, guitars were produced and then the singing and dancing commenced. They dance what they call the 'twist' – seems I heard of that once, long ago and far away. The local version is danced with enthusiasm and much hilarity, especially when some of the older or more exhibitionist people take to the floor. Within moments of the music beginning, a girl came and asked me to dance. Horror of horrors, there was nobody else on the floor but I could not refuse with everybody watching. So I danced. My friend, Tataake, the parliamentary member for Washington, must have taken pity on me as he promptly rose and asked one of the young girls to dance. All in all a very good time was had by all, myself included.

A few words about my new house. It is as big as a barn (a very big barn) and is right on the beach. I mean that literally. From where I sit now, watching the constantly breaking surf, I could throw a stone into the water without difficulty. I'm told that the beach shifts seasonally and that some years they have to sandbag the house to keep water out of the ground floor. The ground floor is just a storage area, the living quarters being all upstairs. The house was built just after the First World War to house six European employees. Thus, it originally had six bedrooms upstairs with kitchen and bathroom downstairs. What used to be a wide veranda has been closed in with glass louvres and made part of the house. As I sit at my table looking out through the louvres, the next speck of land in that direction is Canton in the Phoenix Islands. The surf breaking on the reef below my window is a hissing roar with no beginning and no end.

Saturday November 10th

Another day, another party. A women's church association invited me to their anniversary celebration. It started at 11:30 with mounds of food as always. Then music and dancing and I think I danced with all of the R.A.K. members. These are all older (and some very old), married women who, if they have to face me in the office (as on pay day), are painfully shy for the most part. Not so on the dance floor with all of their friends around them, they're outrageous. One even patted my bum as we danced the twist, which brought forth gales of laughter. This from a woman old enough (almost) to be my mother who would hardly look me in the eye in the office. After dancing, and I danced with young girls too, there were a couple of bible stories acted out by the women and then some hymn singing. I was presented with the inevitable mat and the party came to a close at about 17:00.

One very embarrassing thing happened. During the hymn singing, people began going up to a table and depositing contributions for the R.A.K.. As manager and wealthiest man on the island, I would be expected to contribute handsomely. I had no money with me! Not a cent! I never carry any money, I have no need to as there's nothing to spend it on. I played dumb and when Tabeaua comes to fix dinner, I'll send him along with a contribution. Tabeaua just came in and I sent him with an envelope containing $5. My conscience is salved. I gave Tabeaua the evening off and think I'll have dinner out of the whisky bottle tonight.

During the week, another association, the A.T.N.T., had a welcoming party for me. I think it was Tuesday evening. It started at 19:00 with food and then, when Tataake said there would be entertainment, I said jokingly "bring on the dancing girls", and they did!! Ten girls dancing in formation doing traditional Gilbertese dances. It was great. Of course, afterwards came the inevitable 'twist' and the presentation of the mat. I now have three of them and soon I'll have to start putting them on the floor, beautiful though they are.

Yesterday, Friday, was a holiday (National Day). Monday is also a holiday (Prince Charles' birthday of all things). To me it just means a little peace and quiet in which to get some work

done. I spent three hours on the radio yesterday with Bill, getting advice on the books. I'm afraid most of his advice confused me more than helped me. I presently have all of the books spread out on two tables here in the house and I'm struggling through them. Damn, it's a lot harder than pounding nails. At least the payroll, which amounts to more than 70 people, is now up to date and correct.

Sunday November 11th

Yesterday evening at 20:30, after several drinks, I wended my way down to the protestant church youth club maneaba for 'Island Night'. They have a tape player for music and all of the young people get together and dance. My arrival caused some surprise and amusement. Their small stock of tapes consisted of some local music and a couple of early Beatles tapes. When they found the Beatles music was more to my taste, they played them over and over and I danced constantly. I tried not to dance with the same girl twice, which wasn't difficult as there were many girls present. Dancing on a concrete floor with bare feet just about wore all the skin off my soles by lights out at 23:00.

When the lights went out, I headed for the house with Tabeaua, in the dark. Soon I found we had two girls along with us and one of them told Tabeaua that she wanted to sleep with me. Not knowing which girl it was and being unable to see in the dark, I suggested that we all go up to the house and have coffee. With the kerosene lamp lit, I recognised her as a girl I'd danced with several times and while she was not the most beautiful girl on the island, she was not unattractive. Also, she was right here, right now and very willing. Fortunately I thought to ask Tabeaua who her father was. Her father is Taberna who used to be Merv Fagg's cook. Knowing that, I also knew that she, Katataake is her name, was Merv's girlfriend. I'm still investigating Merv's death and last Thursday I questioned the local policeman. Next week I plan to question Katataake as she was the last one to see Merv alive. On top of all this, I'm sending her father and his whole family off of the island on the next ship. He got into Merv's liquor more than once and on two occasions was locked up overnight by the police. He broke a window screen and broke down a door and he's reported to have threatened to kill Merv on one occasion. Obviously I couldn't get tangled up with Katataake so sent her home and went to bed alone.

Monday November 19th

Today is cash advance day and I'm writing this in between paying out the money spread out on my desk. It's a grey, overcast day with strong gusty winds and I'm keeping an eye on the salvage team as they've moved the tug and could be preparing to pull out. If the weather deteriorates and they go back to Fanning, I have to get Tetaake on board before they leave. Last Friday, the catholic church had a welcome party for me. Food, singing and traditional Gilbertese dancing in traditional costume, including grass skirts. The inevitable 'twist', speeches and presentation of no, not a mat, I was given a beautiful hand-woven basket and a hat (which I wouldn't be seen wearing). Saturday morning I got up early and went out to the tug for a visit. Tabeaua and Bareaka dropped me off and then took the boat to do some fishing, at my request.

On Friday afternoon I'd had some men go out and collect some sprouted coconuts and some green drinking nuts for the Fijian crew. There were about a dozen sacks and they were much appreciated. After coffee and fruit juice on the tug, Skip and I took a boat over to the barge so I could have a look at the operation. So far they have about 400 tons aboard out of a total of 1,000 tons available. We have been supplying six men each day since last Monday to work on the barge, stacking lead. At 10:30, Tabeaua and Bareaka picked me up from the barge. They had several small tuna and kingfish and a good-sized barracuda. I gave half of the fish to Bareaka and, from my half, sent a large chunk to the nurse, Mokura, an admirable lady. The rest of the weekend passed as does most of my leisure time, in beer, books and bed.

Wednesday November 21st

I'm sitting in the office 07:30 and the sun isn't yet high enough to clear the treetops. Everything is wet from last night's torrential rain and the road outside the office is a succession of ankle-deep pools in which the baby pigs cavort.

Thirty feet from where I sit, a very fat lady, naked to the waist, is scrubbing her children under a tap that projects 3 feet out of the ground. As she works, her pendulous breasts swing wildly batting the kids about the head and shoulders. Twenty years ago, most of the women and girls would have been bare-breasted but now it's only the old and ugly ones.

Last Monday, the seas got up to where the salvage team stopped work and the tug and small boat moved around into the lee of the island for the night. By yesterday morning things had calmed down and they were back at work. If the weather holds for them and they don't have to go to Fanning for shelter, then I may be waiting until February for mail.

Monday November 26th

I just checked back and found that it's four months to the day since I last got mail. I talked to Bill by radio (as I do most days) and he tells me that Marty arrived at Fanning Island yesterday and he has a large quantity of mail for me. It may be a long time yet until we can get it here though. The weather is still holding for the salvage team and no word on when the next ship may call here. I'm just about up to date on the books now but it's time to start preparing the November payroll and then the November returns. Still, it beats cutting copra for $3 a day. Tabeaua and Bareaka went out fishing on Saturday morning in the company boat. They came in with 2 tuna, 2 peiri, a kingfish, a barracuda, an unknown and a good story about the one that got away. They had hooked a large tuna and had it almost to the boat when a shark appeared and swallowed it whole. Tabeaua says that its head was so large he would have been unable to encircle it with his arms and Bareaka puts its length at something over 12 feet. That's a big shark! I wanted to know why they didn't bring it in with them and was surprised when they told me that they tried but it broke the line.

Yesterday afternoon, I took a walk along the beach for about two miles and back. This morning my legs are stiff. I'm getting far too little exercise but maybe now that I'm over the hump with the office work I'll get out and about more. This morning I fired my two house girls, Mamelle and Eretia. They have (or had) the softest jobs on the island but they still abuse it. They sit around and knock off early whenever they think I won't notice and they only clean the parts of the house that they think I will see.

Tuesday November 27th

I'll get my mail this afternoon. Marty is going to fly over and drop it from his plane, now that's what I call airmail! He's not making the trip just for me though. The salvage crew had him bring some things down from Honolulu and they're paying him $200 to bring them from Fanning Island to Washington. There being no airstrip here, he'll just fly low and dump them overboard at the back of my house.

Thursday November 28th

Marty's air drop was a real hit with the people here. They all know (of) him and as he flew over, there were shouts of "Marty, Marty" by kids and adults. He made three low passes (less than 100 feet) and dropped packages on each pass. At the end of each run there was thunderous applause. We got aspirin for the hospital, new bed sheets for my house, some papers from Bill, packages for the salvage crew and, most importantly of all, my mail. Janie sent the November 'Pacific Yachting' which contains an article all about me. I got letters from my parents, Terry (my little brother), Maureen (my big sister), Auntie, Janice, Laura and Gordon. Gordon finally married Jan.

Yesterday the salvage team did some blasting to clear part of the wreck. The explosion threw up a spout of water, shook the whole house and killed thousands of fish. When Bareaka came ashore with his men at 18:00, he had more than 1,000 small fish in the boat. As the sun set, we divided them up into 90 piles and each family got more than a dozen fish.

Tueday December 4th

Yesterday was pay day so now I have work to keep me busy again for a few days. I'm trying to collect some of the money owed to the company and also to try and reduce some of the huge copra shortages. Some families got very little money and I felt like Scrooge. Last Saturday morning I went out fishing with Tabeaua and Bareaka. We circumnavigated the island, catching 2 tuna and 2 barracuda, one of which was nearly 4 feet long. Saturday evening I went out to the tug for dinner and a social evening. I stayed the night out there and Bareaka brought me ashore the next morning.

Wednesday December 5th

It's pouring with rain and I'm at a standstill. Not because of the rain but because the first thing I need to start on the books are the trade and ration store figures. Beiata brought me the book yesterday but I promptly discovered some unbelievable discrepancies and sent him back with them to check his figures.

I have a new house girl who started work yesterday. The new girl is young, pretty and energetic and I couldn't have done better if I had chosen her myself (which I did). I couldn't afford to choose a girl openly as people would assume that I'd fired the other girls because I desired the new one (bad for my image). Tabeaua was reluctant to choose one for the same reason (he's engaged to be married). I asked Taukaban to choose a girl but, by certain stipulations and careful engineering, I got the girl I wanted with no one any the wiser. I must stress that while I admit to desiring this girl's body, this in no way influenced my firing of the others.

I have to go out in the rain now as I have my daily radio schedule with Bill in a few minutes and the radio room is on the ground floor of the house.

Saturday December 8th

This morning we were trolling for tuna with three lines rigged with lures made locally out of chicken feathers. The two with me in the boat were Bareaka and his brother-in-law Maerere. We had already caught more than a dozen fine tuna and were considering heading for the offshore bank to catch a shark or two, when I had a strike. Bareaka stopped the engine and he and Maerere had started pulling in their lines so that they wouldn't foul mine, when suddenly, quite close to the boat, the biggest fish I had ever seen leapt clear out of the water and fell back with a splash. We looked at each other stunned as we had all seen the line trailing from its mouth and knew that this beautiful monster was what I had hooked. It was a pacific blue marlin about 9 feet long and weighing 400 pounds and, as we watched, it leapt again and again. At times it would rise up out of the water and by violently thrashing its tail, would remain poised with more than three quarters of its length above the surface. By the time we had gathered our scattered wits, the marlin had also recovered from its panic and the fight was on.

We barely had time to attach Bareaka's hand line to mine to lengthen it before the marlin sounded. It took the line out so fast that I had difficulty in controlling it without burning my hands but finally the sheer length of the line slowed it and turned its head. We spent 3 hours fighting that fish. When I started to tire, I handed the line to Bareaka who handed it on to Maerere, who handed it back to me. We also cheated by using the outboard motor to prevent the marlin from towing us out to sea and also to manoeuvre it into shallower water where it could not dive so deep.

At the end of the 3 hours, the marlin had fought itself to death. The line suddenly started coming in more readily and soon our fish appeared beside the boat. As it came alongside, it rolled over and I sank the fishing spear into its head but, by this time, it had already given up and did not even quiver.

We now had a dead fish on our hands that weighed almost as much as the three of us combined! We didn't even consider bringing it aboard as, even if we could, it would have made the boat too heavy to land through the surf. So, we attached a rope to its tail and towed it ignominiously ashore. As we waited, watching the surf to pick our time to land, we prepared the line to run free. As we made our run in, Maerere paid out the line and when we hit the beach, he left the boat handling to Bareaka, me and our shore crew. As we picked up the boat and ran up the beach to avoid the next wave, Maerere hauled in our marlin at the end of its leash.

Once we had it on the beach, the others were in favour of cutting it up there and then as it was too heavy to move easily.

However, I was adamant that it be carried up to my house so that we could string it up properly by its tail and take real sports fisherman-like photographs. It took four of us to carry it to the house and once there, we ran a rope up to the first floor and, with a bit of heaving and shouting, we got the marlin satisfactorily strung and took the obligatory photos.

Half of a fillet from one side of the fish filled my paraffin-powered freezer with enough left over to make more salt dried fish than I was likely to eat in a long time. After my partners had taken all that they could use, the rest of the marlin and all of the tuna was given away to our appreciative helpers.

Thursday December 13th

It is 07:15 and pouring with rain once more. It rained much of yesterday and all of the day before. I had only half a day's work to last me all week and stretch it as I may, I still had it finished yesterday morning. I spent the rest of yesterday reading a book in the office but I think that is bad for my image so today I'll write instead, it looks more business-like. Tabeaua just came over in the pouring rain with a thermos of hot water and made my coffee. The salvage team were all finished by the weekend and on Sunday, began retrieving moorings. They finished that by Monday afternoon and then about 20 of them came ashore. Skip and Ian didn't make it as they were very busy and the others only got to stay ashore for an hour or so. Takee was taken out to the Salmur just after sunset for transportation to Fanning and thence, with Marty to Christmas Island. Takee has gangrene in his foot and is in bad shape. I had a look at his foot last weekend and the flesh is black, split and stinking. I doubt that they will save the limb even if they save his life. He is also a diabetic. Salmur left on Monday evening and Salvor and barge left on Tuesday morning bound for Kingman reef for a look at a Japanese fishing boat aground there.

08:00 and the rain has stopped. Beiata rang the bell and people are now drifting in to work. Tokibara, my clerk, just arrived and I hardly recognised him. He was wearing a shirt!

Monday December 17th

The sky is fairly clear and the sun is shining but water standing in ankle-deep pools gives mute testimony to a wet weekend.

Yesterday and today, the surf has been higher than I'd hitherto seen. Saturday was spent fishing with Bareaka and Tabeaua and we did very well. There was a large school of tuna feeding off the north coast of the island. The water boiled as they dashed about in a frenzy and a flock of birds darkened the sky overhead as they held position above the feeding fish and picked up the scraps. With 3 lines astern, we would cross beneath the birds and 3 fish would hit at the same moment. At times one or two would break loose (or "fall down" as Tabeaua says) but on at least two occasions we were able to land our hat trick without tangling the lines too badly. Once brought alongside, the hapless fish is speared through the gills, hauled aboard, beaten about the head with a wooden club, unhooked and tossed up into the bow. A quick look around to spot the telltale flock of birds and the chase is on again. Tabeaua's lure was taken by a tuna which was in turn taken by a shark.

We finished the day with 23 yellow fin tuna, the largest being close to 100 pounds, 2 skipjack tuna, one of which Bareaka and I ate before we got ashore and the 6 foot shark that Tabeaua didn't mean to catch. I wore a heavy leather glove on my right hand this time and was thus able to take the pace. By the time we were finished, my arms were ready to drop off and the surf had started to build. Bareaka decided the boat was too heavy to beach through the surf so we handed a large fish to a man who swam out through the surf and Tabeaua jumped overboard with a fish in each hand. Bareaka took us in beautifully on the crest of a wave but just as the boat hit the beach and I jumped into knee-deep water, a cross wave hit us broadside, hurling the boat up and along the beach in a welter of foam. With water foaming over my head and into the boat, I clung to the gunwale and then the wave receded, leaving us on the beach. After hauling all of the fish up to my house, I took out my camera and recorded the occasion for posterity. Between us, we took care of 10-12 fish and then gave the rest away. Tabeaua worked until 19:00 cutting up fish, then made supper (raw fish in coconut cream and lemon juice with rice), then a water pipe burst in the kitchen flooding the floor! Tabeaua took the opportunity to scrub the floor and worked cheerfully through until 21:30.

Thursday December 27th

"And so this is Christmas and what have we done. Another year over and a new one just begun".....

I received many present of mats, hats, baskets and seven embroidered pillow cases with my name on them. I gave gifts of tobacco as everybody smokes and I'm no good with a needle. Most of the gifts arrived on Christmas Eve and I spent all of

Christmas day alone in the house drinking. One strange incident on Christmas morning. Terabota, my house girl, arrived to put fresh flowers on the tables as she does every day. She gave me a present and I gave one to her. As I handed it to her, I bent to kiss her on the cheek and she sprang back as if I had tried to cut her throat. I was shocked to discover from Tabeaua later in the day that Gilbertese people don't kiss. In moments of great passion, they rub noses but affection is never, ever shown in public. I've never seen a Gilbertese couple so much as hold hands. It puts paid to any designs I had on these dusky island maidens. How could you make love to a girl without kissing her? Oh well, only another year to wait.

The whole plantation has been on holiday since the 21st and doesn't resume work until January 2nd. Last Saturday we had planned to go fishing but the surf was too high. Instead we took the launch along the canal to the lake to fish there. Well, it rained and rained, the fish weren't biting, the launch engine began to misbehave and it rained some more. You might say the day's fishing was a wash out. At midnight of the same day, we set out to do some reef fishing by lamplight. With Tilly lamp in one hand and net in the other, you wade through the shallows over the reef scooping up small fishes and crayfish. Unfortunately, we got only two crayfish but a multitude of other little fish. It rained for much of the time and we got home tired and wet at 04:00.

On Monday, we were out on the ocean despite strong winds. If you have a fish on the line and a shark takes it, the Gilbertese people say that you must have slept badly the night before. I must have slept very badly because that happened to me three times. Each time I would be hauling in a small tuna and it would suddenly turn into a big shark. The first one ran out some line then spat out the hook. The second took out all of the line and I couldn't even slow it down. I had a heavy leather glove on my right hand and though it was wet, the line burned my hand. The end of the line was secured to the boat and when all of the slack was gone, the monster almost turned the boat over and then it was gone. When I pulled in all of the line, I found the hook straightened out. The third one we landed. We took turns hauling on the line until we got it to the surface then slipped a noose over its head. We towed it astern for a little way to weaken it, then brought it alongside and held it there while Tabeaua and Bareaka took turns at beating it about the head with a wooden club. Once it was well stunned, Bareaka drove the big knife many times into its head and heart. It was over 7 feet long and about 250 pounds and we had a struggle getting it aboard so, about 50 feet from the beach, we tossed it over the side with a long line tied to its tail then Tabeaua swam in through the surf with the end of the line.

We also had aboard 12 tuna – the sharks didn't get them all. We cut the shark in half on the beach and it still took two men to each half to drag it up to the house. Bareaka's wife and another man then spent about an hour cutting out the jaws for me.

1980!!!

1 minute past midnight and the first New Year I can ever remember seeing in alone. Never mind, the people will be along between now and dawn to wish me a happy one. Tabeaua made about 100 doughnuts and I have 5 boxes of gum to give out.

Wednesday January 9th

I've been back at work since the 2nd with little happening worthy of note. The weather is predominantly dry and sunny, surf variable. I have started stacking copra in earnest, ready for the arrival of the Vili in early February. Basic food lines store are now very low and we have been on ration since October. Vili will be the first ship since last July.

Tuesday January 15th

I went fishing last Saturday despite outrageous surf conditions. Tabeaua claimed to be sick and stayed ashore. Bareaka told me later that Tabeaua confessed to being simply afraid of the surf. We had a very disappointing day catching only 2 barracuda and 2 small fish. There were manta rays out there by the dozen, lazily gliding along the surface on their 6 foot wing span. I had never seen them in such numbers. Maybe they scared off all of the other fish? It was very rough with 6-8 foot swells running and 20 knots of wind. When we closed with the shore at 16:00, we found that the surf had increased and was rolling in at 8-12 feet high. We tied everything to the boat in case we rolled, checked the fuel level and headed in. The only thing that got us ashore safely was Bareaka's superb boat handling. We surfed in on the crest of the final wave and hit the beach with a bump that threw me from my seat. Before the next wave could overwhelm us, many willing hands were laid on the boat and the next wave helped us on our way up the beach. Quite a crowd had turned out to watch and see if we would make it. We were the only boat that had gone out.

That evening we borrowed Biribo's boat, it being smaller and lighter, and set off along the canal to the lake to fish for eels. It was a strange sensation to be slipping along the canal by the light of a pressure lamp being held in the bow. The stars peeping down through the gently rustling palm fronds overhead. The canal always invokes thoughts of Africa to me and I watch hoping to catch a glimpse of a crocodile slipping silently into the water or a hippo showing just eyes and nostrils above water.

On reaching the lake, our speed increased and there was nothing to be seen for some time until the palm trees loomed over us at the far end. A stick, 3-4 feet long with a large barbed hook at the end is employed in eel catching. The eels are found in shallow water near the lake shore and when spotted in the lamp light, they are 'gaffed' with the hook. All very well in theory but we did not see a single eel. For all of our efforts we got a total of 8 very small fish. We got home at around 01:00.

Monday January 21st

My 29th birthday came and went and it is strange to recall that I had a 29th birthday 4 years ago. Days go by with little to report except shop talk and fishing. Many men are working in the settlement now, sacking copra. We've had constant breakdowns with our motor transport and the mechanics have been working flat out patching up our old and rusty trailers to keep them on the road. If we don't get the new trailer we've ordered on the next ship, then the plantation will soon grind to a halt. One day last week, we had all of the trailers break down on the same day and copra cutting ceased. Now we have only two trailers that are roadworthy and the next time a wheel bearing goes, we'll be down to one as we have no more spares. On top of this, my foreman has been off sick for the past two weeks, my copra overseer was off all of last week and my acting foreman is also my head mechanic and has been busy with trailer repairs.

Consequently, I'm having to do all of the supervising around the settlement myself. Imagine trying to supervise 30 or more men spread around 5 locations when only a couple of them speak any English. You might come across 5 men who are supposed to be sewing up sacks, all sitting doing nothing. On enquiring why, they will indicate that they have run out of twine. Naturally nobody would think to come and ask for twine, it's more pleasant to sit in the shade and wait. Not knowing the language, nothing can be said so you simply send somebody for more twine. Variations on this theme continue all over.

I just got back from a walk around the place. Eight men were busy stacking sacks of second-grade copra in the wrong place. Eight men are now busy moving it all to the right place. Enough shop talk, now for fishing.....

Last Saturday dawned with little surf and partly clear (or partly cloudy) skies. Plenty of tuna about and within an hour or so we had six of them. As I hauled in the 7th, I decided it must be the biggest yet and when I got it to the surface, I found it had turned into a large shark with several small sharks keeping it company. As soon as it realised that my intentions were malicious, it took off and had most of the line out before I turned its head. In the meantime, Bareaka and Tabeaua quickly baited the big shark hooks and even more quickly caught two smaller sharks. By the time I'd retrieved some of my line, they had those aboard and had hooked two more. By the time those were aboard, I had mine near the surface and we could see it was a monster. I had to play it carefully as I was using 250 pound nylon line and a tuna hook and I've had hooks that size straighten out. Bareaka prepared a noose in one of the shark lines and we got that over its head when it flailed the water and caught me a mighty blow on the shoulder with its tail. We towed it, beat it and then held it alongside while I did as much damage as I could to its brain box with the big knife.

Bareaka then shoved an oar down its throat (it was the blade end and it went in a good 4 feet) and beat it over the head with the club for several minutes. By the time we got it aboard, the boat was very low in the water and all of the lines were a tangled mess. We were back ashore by 10:30. It had taken about an hour to land the shark. It was about the same size as the last big one, 7 feet and 250 pounds. In the afternoon I cut out its jaws for drying.

Monday February 11th

Three weeks have passed since I last wrote and today's news is very sad. I had a scheduled call with Bill at 10:00 but Marty came on instead to say that Bill had disappeared. He was last seen around midnight on Saturday by his wife Marina and when she awoke at 06:00, Bill had not been to bed and he was not in the house. A flashlight was missing and he had evidently gone for a nocturnal stroll. A search was conducted all day Sunday but no trace of him was found. None of the boats were missing and he could not have walked far which means that he must be in the ocean. The tide was running out from midnight on and he would have been carried many miles out to sea. Bill's health has not been good recently and he has been very depressed. Nothing has been going right for him of late and the lack of shipping, lack of stores, lack of concise communications and apparent lack of concern from the company have been topped off by an unpleasant labour dispute over the lack of food.

I'm pushing the idea of accidental death although I personally do not doubt that Bill took his own life. He was not given to midnight strolls and if he were, he'd have no reason to go to the edge of the pass. The deciding factor though is the keys. Bill always, always carried his keys with him (as do I) but on Saturday night, he left them in the house when he went out. I've sent a telegram to Sydney suggesting that I go to Fanning Island aboard a fishing boat that will call here next week.

Monday February 18th

The fishing boat carrying emergency stores to Washington and Fanning Islands should be here by Thursday and I will get a ride down to Fanning. This idea has been confirmed by Head Office. A Mr and Mrs Kates are presently on Fanning Island. They have been employed by the company to do a detailed study of both islands from a social and agricultural standpoint. Mr Kates has been asked to stand in as manager until a relief can be found but he is leaving the details to me and I'm attempting to run Fanning Island by remote control (radio-generated). The labour dispute is still bad there with employees only working four hours each day and demanding to be paid for eight. I'm presently negotiating directly with union headquarters in Tarawa.

Day to day activities and plantation work are recorded in the plantation log each day and as I will retain the log when I leave here, I see no reason to duplicate everything here. I will resume this log when I leave but in the meantime, I will use it to record any random observations.

August 1980

I started getting sick in early August. Severe chest pains led me to believe that I had another punctured lung. John Brydon and myself decided that I'd better get off the island and on August 15th 1980 a yacht arrived from Fanning Island to pick me up. We had a rough trip and arrived back on Fanning on the evening of the 16th. On the 18th I flew to Christmas Island with Marty and on the 19th I flew from Christmas Island to Honolulu. After tests and x-rays costing $182.00, it was decided that I had pleurisy and that this had been caused by a viral infection , namely denge fever. Nothing very serious and no available treatment, I have to just rest up until it goes away.

On August 22nd, Phil Best, General Manager of Burns Philp arrived in Honolulu and I had two days of talks with him. The company has agreed to sell both islands to Kiribati for $400,000 which is just a token payment. Basically, the government said sell for that price or we'll legislate you out of there, which they apparently could do. Burns Philp is now going to sell the islands and then lease them back to continue running them as plantations. It sounds crazy but at least I still have a job. After talking with Best, I flew to England as I had two weeks to kill before I could connect with a ship from Christmas Island back to Washington Island.

I spent a year and three months on Washington Island which had the reputation of being the least visited, inhabited island in the Pacific. During that time one yacht paid an overnight visit and three ships called. My major contribution to Washington Island was the construction of a 3,000 foot runway enabling the Piper Aztec, that operated on the Line Islands at that time to land there. The runway became operational just one week before I left Washington island.

In January 1981 I returned to Fanning Island as its assistant manager under John Bryden, a Scotsman who had lived in the Gilbert Islands for many years. My main duties were supervision in the field and the construction of roads and causeways to improve efficiency in the collection of copra. During the next two years, $3^{1}/_{2}$ miles of causeway were constructed across tidal flats to link up separate land masses, and many miles of new road were built. All this was to no avail as with the falling price for copra, the islands could not be run without huge losses, and by the end of 1982 Burns Philp had decided to close down both plantations. The Kiribati government had long been campaigning to buy these islands from Burns Philp and the sale was finalised on the 31st March 1983. By this time John Bryden had already left to start a car hire business on Christmas Island, some 180 miles away, catering to a small but steady tourist industry there.

Since the only retail store on Fanning was owned and operated by Burns Philp I now came under pressure from the people and the government to take it over as my own business so that the service could continue. Since nobody else had the capital or the expertise to run such an operation I somewhat reluctantly approached Burns Philp who readily agreed to sell me the remaining stock on hand at a more than reasonable price, and also offered much assistance in the importing of new supplies. Overnight I became a self employed businessman and sole importer for Fanning Island.

Though the business never made me more than a bare living, the lifestyle was quite pleasant. I employed a storeman who did the actual counter work, a house girl to do laundry and cleaning, a cook and a young fellow as general dogsbody. My house was the largest in the village and I had my own self contained electrical and water supplies that I had installed. I owned a power boat for fishing offshore and a flat-bottomed dinghy for net fishing in the lagoon. Balandra sat forlornly up on the land beside my back door raising feelings of guilt every time I looked at her decaying woodwork and grubby hull.

As all good things must come to an end, so too did my comfortable life on Fanning Island. I became involved in a complex dispute with the Kiribati Government who were my landlords. Part of the dispute was their claim that I owed back rent on my house to the tune of $10,661.45 due to an error on their part when assessing the property. I had been paying rent of $31.00 per month which was in line with what everyone else was paying, but now they said my rent should have been $355.00 per month and that I must pay the difference retroactive for $2^1/_2$ years! At the same time I was advised that my business licenses and residents permit would not be renewed for 1986 and it became clear that I was being ousted to make room for a government-sponsored co-operative store which had recently opened on Fanning Island.

Sadly, I began to rebuild Balandra, replacing her rotten cabin and decking with timber from old packing cases and pallets for want of anything better. On 30th December 1985 I had her in the water and was ready to depart but, at the last minute, the police constable arrived, seized my passport and told me that his instructions were to prevent me from leaving Fanning Island until I had handed over the disputed back rent.

18:00 Saturday 4th January 1986

I am at sea, about 300 miles from Fanning Island and bound for Pago Pago, American Samoa. It is blowing about 30 knots out of the east and I'm headed south through large and confused seas. The decks are mostly awash and everything below is wet due to numerous deck leaks. I've only the reefed main up and we're probably making 3-4 knots with the new wind vane steering. The motion of the boat is pretty wild and it is hard to write with the log on my lap and my body wedged athwartships. The poor old body is getting pretty bruised and scraped up as I try to go about my business inside this wild, wet box.

I managed to get a dubious sight around noon and a worse one around 14:00. The resulting fix put me about 10 miles north of the equator. So, maybe I just crossed the equator, or maybe I'm just about to or, who knows, maybe I'm on it right now. So what, right! For the record, I'm also around 164° W! Today is my fifth day at sea and I should give a brief rundown of the voyage so far.

23:00 Monday December 30th 1985

John, from the yacht 'Skye II' rowed me across the pass to where Balandra was moored. She was basically ready for sea as I should have left this morning. When the tide turned at midnight, I slipped out of the pass under sail with a half moon to light my way. Once clear of the pass I went hell for leather on the fastest course with too much sail up as I feared pursuit.

By 02:00 I was well clear and dropped the jenny and reefed the main. It was blowing about 20 knots out of the south east and I left Balandra to steer herself away from the island. I was sick and exhausted and curled up down below amongst cartons of good not yet stowed. I had slept little the night before and the day had been one of anxiety and strain. I've never felt so bad on a passage as on that first night. The boat could have sunk under me and I wouldn't have cared. I was tired to exhaustion, nauseas and sick at heart. I had left Fanning Island after all of those years but worse than that, I had been forced to sneak away like a thief in the night and to sail with neither clearance nor passport. What will become of me now. I slept fitfully until dawn of the 31st and rose feeling poorly.

19:30 Sunday January 5th

I'm nearing the end of my sixth day and we have good news and bad news. The strong wind continued through last night and I got little sleep as I was tossed around in my wet bed. We continued jogging along slowly all night and this morning with just the reefed main and, in the 24 hours to noon today, made only 50 miles. At around noon, the wind went down a little and shifted to the east, north east. The seas have now gone down some and with the wind abaft the beam, the motion is much easier and there's less water coming on deck. We're now heading south under full main and jib and making good speed. The bad news is that Balandra is leaking!! I don't mean drips through the deck but a serious hull leak which we've never experienced before. It's not yet cause for alarm being about 2-3 gallons per hour. The leak is back by the rudder post and is inaccessible at this time. I would have to take a lot of stuff out of the aft hatch and then crawl in there, head first. It can't be done unless the sea calms down. I just have to keep bailing.

December 31st was fairly smooth sailing which was just as well as I was very tired. The wind was around 15-20 knots on a broad reach with the jenny and main up. By noon of January 1st, the wind had gone more northerly and I put up the twin headsails. We ran with these before a strong (20 knot) wind through until the morning of the 2nd, by which time the wind had gone back to east, south east and was blowing lustily. Through the 2nd and 3rd of January, we kept working southward through large and breaking seas with just the reefed main. Wet, nasty and tiring.

19:30 Monday January 6th

Well, things are much improved. Last night was terrible. I had to get up every hour or so to bail and my bed was sopping. 05:30 found me shivering naked in the cockpit waiting for the sun to rise. At first light I took down the main and hoisted the twin jibs. The wind is still a good 20 knots and the seas large but with it all from astern, the motion is easier.

I decided I had to try and locate and fix the leak. There is no way I could bail like that for two weeks. I pulled everything out of the aft hatch and piled it in the cockpit. I was then able to get my head and shoulders in there and found the leak under the aft end of the cockpit. I could see it but couldn't reach it. I then pulled everything out of the starboard quarter berth from inside the boat. The quarter berths are the size of coffins, thin men's coffins, and the end I had to get my head and shoulders into was the foot end. I reached the leak and plugged it with a piece of wood caulked with bubblegum and hammered home as best I could with two and a half inches to swing the hammer. The leak is fixed. It took all day doing this then re-stowing everything. I got the foam bedding, sheets, pillows etc. strung in the rigging for a few hours of sun and wind (and spray of course). Tonight my bed will be damp but not wet and I'm going to sleep and sleep.

We ran 98 miles from noon to noon today which is pretty good. We're moving well now with the twins still set and steering. Those huge breaking seas come roaring down from astern and Balandra just lifts her little tail and up we go, scooting along on their crests and then we get left behind waiting for the next one. Sleep time.

19:30 Tuesday January 7th

I slept from 21:00 last night until 07:30 this morning and feel much better. I woke briefly at 05:00, long enough to check the compass beside me and listen to the wind for a moment. We're still trucking right along with the wind at about 20 knots from the east, north east. We covered 120 miles from noon to noon which is terrific. It leaves us about 700 miles to go with 600 miles covered. Mind you, we sailed a lot more than 600 miles to get here. We're a little further west than I care for and I've now hauled the twins around as far as I can so we have the wind on our port quarter. It's hard to say what compass course we're on as she wanders outrageously with the twins steering but we'll see tomorrow what course we've made good. Pago bears 210° true from our noon position.

I had a shower and shave in the cockpit and did laundry today i.e. dragged my shorts and t-shirt at the end of a rope for a while. All of my clothes are packed in plastic bags except for this one ragged t-shirt and shorts. At the end of the passage they'll go overboard. The bedding foam is still damp and will probably remain so. There is too much spray at deck level and they're too bulky to hoist aloft. I did little else today but eat and read and now it's bedtime again.

15:00 Wednesday January 8th

A rain squall woke me last midnight and I was obliged to leave my bed and go naked into the rain. The wind and seas had picked up dramatically and Balandra could not hold her course unaided. We had been running with the twin headsails set and steering and the wind coming over our port quarter. Rather than change sails, I decided to take the helm until the squall passed. Freeing the jib sheets from the tiller, I made them fast with the jibs fairly slack to spill wind.

With the sails set and Balandra on her course, I settled myself at the helm and began to notice my surroundings. The sky was black with no moon or star and my entire being existed within the range of the masthead strobe light. This flashed like lightning on the nearby whitecaps with a monotony broken only by the irregularity of the waves. The torrential rain stirred up the phosphorescence around the boat adding glimmers of blue and green to the starkness of black and white light and Balandra's wake shimmered. I became aware of beams of white light dancing over the waves and realised that I had left the interior light on. As Balandra pitched and rolled, light from the four inch porthole on each side flickered forth in a narrow beam.

Balandra drove onwards with rain and spray streaming from her decks. As I sat at the helm I was remotely aware of the safety harness chafing my wet skin but nothing could detract from the night's dreamlike quality. How long was I on the helm? One hour, two? The wind began to falter then dropped as rapidly as it had risen. The rain slackened to no more than a fine drizzle and I began to feel cold. With little wind to guide them, the waves began to tumble about and jostle each other but, after re-rigging the jib sheets to the tiller, I found the wind was sufficient to hold Balandra on her course. Going below and drying my body, I made coffee from hot water in the thermos flask. On checking my watch, I found that the squall had lasted for over three hours.

At 05:00 the wind returned and I rose to adjust the sails and then awaited the sunrise. Another good day's run with 110 miles until noon today though still too far to the west. Tomorrow, at first light I'll drop the twins and raise the main and jenny (weather permitting) and drive due south for a day or two to put us back on course. With chores completed and more than half of the passage done, I decided to open <u>the</u> bottle of wine. I spent half an hour looking and still couldn't find the damn corkscrew. I know it is on board somewhere. Well hell! I opened the bottle by picking the cork out with a screwdriver. Of course I cannot now re-cork it or indeed even set it down. I now have pen in one hand and bottle in the other. Goodnight.

19:00 Thursday January 9th

120 miles to noon today! Before sunrise I had struck the twins and hoisted the jenny and reefed main. We now have the wind abeam and are headed due south. We're moving fast and the motion is not too bad but there's a lot of spray and no way to dry bedding etc. I've got lots of salt water sores on my body from the constant wet, especially my bum. I also have them on elbows, hips and the undersides of my forearms. I also got them under my watchstrap so I've stopped wearing my watch. The white strip of skin thereunder promptly got badly sunburned. All in all, not a very comfortable trip. I saw a ship this afternoon. It came from astern and would have crossed my stern diagonally some two miles back. However, it stopped and just sat there and didn't move again all of the time I had it in sight. Strange.

19:30 Friday January 10th

The wind dropped off during the night and has been around 10-15 knots all day. We still made 115 miles to noon today and now have about 400 miles to go. The wind is just abaft the beam and we're moving along nicely with an easy motion and not much water coming aboard. We had a school of skipjack tuna jumping and feeding around the boat this afternoon for about two hours. They were either going our way or it was a very big school. I saw a plane high overhead going north. Other than that, I've been eating, reading and trying to get things dry.

LITTLE BOAT, BIG OCEAN

19:00 Saturday January 11th

The wind has been 10 knots or less all day although we had a couple of rain squalls last night. We still clocked 110 miles to noon today which surprised me. We have now less than 300 miles to go. The wind is presently very light and we're barely moving. However, there are heavy black clouds to windward and I anticipate more rain squalls. They will, of course, hold off until I'm snug in my bed and it is full black dark (new moon today).

20:00 Sunday January 12th

What a day! We've covered only 70 miles to noon today and I had to work for every one of them. As predicted, the wind picked up at midnight and I had to get up and reef the main. No sooner was I back in bed than it again fell light. Another squall struck at 04:00 from the north and put us on a south east heading. Rather than change sails in the dark, I let it go. I woke again at 06:00 with the boat barely moving south but, as the sky lightened, another squall struck from the north. Instead of changing sails, I took the helm and ran before the wind through boisterous seas for an hour. I've been in the cockpit all day. We've had winds from every point of the compass and I ran the motor for 5-6 hours when there was no wind at all. At about 18:00, a breeze came up from the south and is still holding. We're now moving nicely over calm seas, heading south west. As of noon we have 210 miles to go.

20:00 Monday January 13th

Another slow day with 80 miles made good to noon, most of which was made last night. The wind held well and kept us right on course until first light and then dropped to a whisper. All day we've kept barely slipping along over a calm sea. With so little wind and a clear blue sky, it's been a choice of burning in the sun topsides or being stewed in my own sweat below. At least all of the bedding is now dry.

20:30 Tuesday January 14th

Ti kan roko! (We're almost there!) Only about 60 miles covered to noon today. At 14:00 I sighted land. Not my destination but the Manna Islands. These are part of Samoa but lie 60 miles east of Tutuila Island (Pago). Still, I'm right where I thought I was. It never ceases to amaze me when my celestial navigation gets me to where I want to go. The wind was very light all morning and died right away in the afternoon. We motored for a couple of hours. At about 18:00, a light breeze came up and we're now running slowly with the twins set. About 50 miles to go. I hope tomorrow morning is clear. I saw dolphins today for the first time this trip.

Saturday January 18th

Happy Birthday to me! I phoned home today so that the family could wish me a happy birthday but they were out. Back to the story. I awoke at 03:00 on the morning of the 15th, I could see the lights of Tutuila Island, right where it was supposed to be. However, it took me until 11:00 to close the land and sail around that east end of the island to Pago Pago harbour. I phoned customs and immigration from the clearance dock and they came down to the dock to meet me. They were not at all happy when they found that I had no clearance or passport. I was taken to the Attorney General's office where, after a lot of fast talking, I was given permission to stay for 30 days. However, that was just the beginning. I still had to convince the Chief Immigration Officer, then the Chief Customs office, then the Port Director, then the Harbour Master, each and every one of whom was ready to send me right back out to sea. I didn't get everything squared away until 17:00, by which time I'd told my story at least 20 times. Soon after 17:00, I entered the closest bar (The Seaside Gardens) and sat there until it closed.

On the 16th of January I contacted the British High Commission by phone and it seems like there will be no problem getting a new passport.

I arrived back in England on March 17th via Honolulu and Los Angeles after two months in Samoa.

I finally sold Balandra in Samoa for $1,000 US. A sad day indeed....

LaVergne, TN USA
07 February 2011
215579LV00001B